The Delusion of Passion:
Why Millennials Struggle to Find Success

By David Anderson and Mark Nathan

This book is dedicated to our wives, who inspire us to become more everyday. Their love, respect and commitment is truly humbling.

Table of Contents

About the Authors

David Anderson

Born in 1985, David is currently the CEO of KEEP GLOBAL North America and previously the co-founder of School Loan 411, a student-loan advisory firm. He was inducted as a Global Shaper with The World Economic Forum and is the Senior Advisor to the Honorary Consul to the country of Moldova. David worked in investment banking at Goldman Sachs in New York City and investment management at J.P. Morgan in Chicago. He also worked as an aide at the White House from 2011 to 2012. He is a proud graduate of Chicago State University, where he graduated with Honors, and Harvard University's Explorations Program. He resides with his wife Kristin and young daughter in the Bronzeville neighborhood.

Mark Nathan

Born in 1982, Mark is the child of Burmese and Filipino immigrants. He paid his way through college as an actor and started his life as an entrepreneur, launching a film festival at age twenty-one. Mark has built a number of different businesses, and became financially free at twenty-seven years old. Mark has been invited to speak globally about goal-setting, personal development, team-building, financial freedom and creating culture. Mark is a graduate of Loyola University Chicago and is a proud Chicagoan. He and his wife Meredith live in the South Loop neighborhood of Chicago.

Prologue

David Anderson & Mark Nathan

Perhaps some of this sounds familiar:

- I will yell at you if you haven't seen my favorite movie.
- If I need to learn how to do something, I'll check YouTube.
- I'll buy something for a good cause.
- At least twenty-five percent of the pictures I take on my phone are selfies.
- I've contributed to my friends' projects/causes on Kickstarter or GoFundMe for a number of reasons, but most importantly, because my friends are awesome.
- Playing a video game with downtime is just as good as seeing a movie.
- I've worn a wristband to raise awareness, or left a wristband on for weeks after an event.
- I take pictures of my food.
- I have binge-watched many, many things on Netflix.
- There have been multiple occurrences where I've watched more than thirty minutes of YouTube videos involving cats, dogs, song covers and/or people falling down.
- I have an itch to check my phone every time it makes a noise, even if I know it's not important.
- I know it's wrong, but I have a general disinterest in any pop culture from before I was born.
- I have spent hours on Facebook/Twitter/Instagram doing absolutely nothing.

- I would take a cool experience over some extra cash.
- I'm more impressed by someone with 1,000,000 subscribers on YouTube than by someone with an Ivy League education.
- If I leave my phone at home, it's like I've lost an appendage.
- When I post something funny on social media, I check periodically to see who "liked" or retweeted it.
- When I have very important thoughts (such as, "I wonder what Robert Downey, Jr. has been up to?"), I will search Wikipedia.
- Even if it's the same price, I'd rather take an Uber than a cab, because anything I can do on an app is more awesome.
- I'm secretly proud of myself when I come up with a #cleverhashtag.
- I sometimes text people who are in the same room.

If you connected with two-thirds of these statements, then this book is for you—and for our whole generation.

The two of us writing this book are not PhD's from fancy universities with 20,000 case studies to share with you.

We're not sociologists pouring through hundreds of surveys to compile research.

We're just a couple of guys trying to take over the world, and looking for a few more people to share the journey with.

Millennials

Researchers define generations by assigning catchy titles to ranges of birth years:
The Silent Generation: 1925–1945
Baby Boomers: 1946–1964
Generation X: 1964–1979
and so on...

Researchers use birth years to suggest commonalities between these groups, but the defining characteristic isn't actually your birthday; it's the way you view and interact with the world around you. Growing up in those years meant that you had shared circumstances with your fellow peers that shaped the way you view the world. Similar circumstances produce experiences, which create similar character traits, which produce similar patterns of behavior, which make it easy to use broad generalizations. It's not an exact science, but generations do tend to see the world in a similar way.

Which is why we know it's silly to put birth-year ranges on being a Millennial. You'd look for the year you were born and simultaneously reject the idea that someone is trying to get into your head, all while thinking about a name for our generation that would be way cooler than the one the researchers came up with.

The goal of this book is not to study, label or criticize. Quite the opposite actually. We see nothing but big things for our generation.

Decades from now, we believe that our Millennial generation will have the opportunity to be remembered as The Most Productive Generation in history.

Decades from now, we believe that our Millennial generation will have the opportunity to be remembered as The Most Productive Generation in history. We've been handed more technology than anyone could have dreamed of a few generations ago, which streamlines communication and increases our opportunities to learn. Right now, we can talk to someone on the other side of the world by clicking a button, and we can physically see them in less than twenty-four hours. We have an amazing foundation of education and empowerment that has been provided for us by our parents and previous generations. And more than anything else, we have each other.

9

We have a heart to see each other win.
We have a loyalty to the greater good.
We have passion to do the amazing.
We have a need to accomplish the awesome.
We have an inexplicable desire for world domination.

But for all of these attributes, we're referred to as the Distracted Generation. We're viewed by everyone else as entitled, lazy and not living up to our potential. Parents/teachers/bosses say these things with good intentions—it's a way of letting us know they see a lot of buried talents. But when we hear these statements, it just makes us want to stop listening.

How things were before technology, how hard everyone had to work, how phones and video games are destroying everything natural in the world—these statements are made with the goal to inspire us to want more, but they don't acknowledge that they're already preaching to the choir.

Sure, we could be doing more. But we're not lazy; we're uninspired. We want to find something worth doing, not just find something to do.

Sure, it seems like we're easily distracted. But we don't have ADHD; we're actually pretty focused. Yes, our phone can be a distraction from what's right in front of us, but we actually have seven things going on simultaneously...it's all just happening on one device.

Sure, it seems like we're indecisive. But we're really weighing options; we're trying to figure out how to fit three lifetimes into one.

What we need isn't a lecture, but rather the right mindset. We're close, but we might be just a little bit off...

What we need isn't a lecture, but rather the right mindset.

~

1° Off

I (Mark) recently traveled to Australia from Chicago to speak at a conference, and over the course of two weeks, flew to several different cities. The flight itinerary included: Chicago to LA, LA to Sydney, Sydney to Melbourne, and Melbourne to Adelaide. In order of the length of each flight, it looked like this:

Melbourne to Adelaide: 1 hour and 15 minutes
Sydney to Melbourne: 2 hours
Chicago to LA: 4 hours
LA to Sydney: 14 hours

Obviously, every flight starts with a charted and efficient plan to the final destination. But what if, upon take-off, the plane was 1° off course? Let's say the autopilot was off, the real pilots didn't notice, and everyone just assumed their original plan was solid.

On one of the shorter flights to Adelaide or Melbourne, 1° off wouldn't be a major problem. You'd probably end up in a different part of the city, but it would be nothing more than a small detour that a little extra time couldn't fix. There would be a delay as you corrected your course, but nothing too dramatic would happen.

On a medium-sized flight, like the four-hour flight from Chicago to LA, if you were 1° off from the start, it would create a much bigger problem. You wouldn't just end up in a different part of the city; you would find yourself in a different part of the state! There would need to be some significant changes to your plans for arrival!

On a longer trip, like the 14 hours from LA to Sydney, 1° off the charted course would create a catastrophe! You wouldn't just end up in a different part of the state, you would end up in an entirely different continent (or worse yet, in the middle of the ocean)! After the fourteen-hour flight, you'd find yourself nowhere close to your planned destination and would be a completely different trip altogether.

You had grand intentions with a great plan, but that 1° off put you nowhere close to where you had intended to be.

The "1° off" principle is simply this — the further you plan to go, the more damaging 1° off becomes.

That is what's happening right now to our entire generation. We're 1° off and we don't realize it. There are big things we want to accomplish and we want to get there yesterday, but we might be starting just a little off track and not even know it.

The further you want to go in life, the more important it is to get started correctly. The more you want to accomplish, the more you need to check your course along the way. Our generation has no shortage of big things we want to accomplish, but that 1° off could make a pretty big difference if we want to succeed in accomplishing those big things!

The further you want to go in life, the more important it is to get started correctly.

1° Off: Wanting More vs. Wanting the Most

If we move this "1° off" principle from fiction into real life, you'll see how far off course someone can get and not even know!

Let's take the phrase, "I want more out of life." It's a pretty common sentiment that I think most can agree with. It sounds inspiring...like something successful people would say. Telling people that you want more out of life is a simple way to let people know you're looking to do more and that you have the desire for bigger things.

The problem is that the phrase is vague. I want more out of life — what does that mean? How do I get more out of life?

Wanting more out of life sounds like something you can achieve with a couple of promotions at your job or earning a little more money this year. Maybe "wanting more" means you'll be happy when you finally learn to play the guitar or bench-press 250 pounds? Perhaps wanting more is an itch that can be scratched with an extra vacation or a slightly nicer place to live?

What if we adjusted that phrase just one degree in a different direction? Instead of wanting *more* out of life, what if we wanted THE MOST out of life? Wanting THE MOST out of life is a mindset; it's understanding that your life is a journey, a constant exploration of who you are and what you have to offer the world, a struggle between the person you are and the person that you could be.

Wanting THE MOST out of life means that you don't subscribe to the false notion that your best days are somehow slipping away from you. It's understanding that the best days of your life are decades away! That doesn't mean that the life you're living right now is miserable. Today is exhilarating because it's the foundation for tomorrow.

Wanting THE MOST out of life means that *every* experience you have can and should be the best moment of your life...so far. A wedding is not the beginning of a slow decline; it should be the best day of a relationship up to that point! Every relationship should be on a steady incline, because you're both doing your best to make the most out of every day, and you're doing it together.

It's a very big difference when you simply switch from wanting more out of life to wanting THE MOST out of life. Really, you were only 1° off, but a lifetime of wanting more could leave you desperately short of what you actually desired: a lifetime of wanting the MOST.

Don't be fooled...

Don't be fooled by the title of this book. As you'll see in the following pages, we wholeheartedly believe in the importance of living with passion in your life. In fact, we think it's so important that we have dedicated this entire book to making sure that our generation, with all of its endless promise and potential, doesn't live an entire life 1° off course—and as a result, miss the boat on passion entirely.

We hope this book can help you with some small course correction—the type that has made a big difference for us. We hope this book can help you make great decisions and accomplish so much that you really can fit three lifetimes into one.

We hope this book can help you create a life that you will be truly passionate about living.

Introduction for David Anderson
Mark Nathan

One of the best things in life is spending time with high-achievers. They have an enthusiasm for life and energy that makes you certain that you too can accomplish big things. It's not a question of *if* life has gotten better since the last time you saw him/her, the only question is *how* much is life better. That's why I love spending time with David Anderson.

I first met David through a mutual friend when he was nineteen years old. His wide smile and goofy laugh made him instantly memorable. He was drawn to my friends and to me—all of us in our early to mid-twenties, wanting the most out of life and doing something about it. He was balancing a lot, and as I found out through some late night chats and car rides home, he actually had much more on his plate than most people his age.

Dave's mom was diagnosed with schizophrenia, making her unreliable as a parent and role model for his younger siblings. He didn't come from a family of means, but he had the spirit and the drive to accomplish at a high level. As he was a budding entrepreneur, he ascertained that the most financially lucrative way to move ahead in his neighborhood was to become a drug dealer. Thankfully, he had enough smarts to prepare for a life that was much bigger than this.

After several life-altering experiences, Dave started working at Goldman Sachs and JP Morgan doing finance and wealth management in his early twenties. He has definitely seen how much money is out there and how the "other half" lives. He was also chosen from tens of thousands of applicants for an internship at the White House with the Barack Obama administration, where he quickly became an aide and gained some very rare access. Very few people get a chance to be behind closed doors for meetings and decisions where the stakes are so high.

This is where you get to really see David Anderson. Many would come out of that experience bragging about all the amazing people they met, or talking about how much this experience could accelerate their career. But in typical Dave fashion, the first thing he wanted to do was talk about the best ways to start really affecting change in this amazing country. As he was launching his first traditional business, it was never about chasing the money; it was about doing something he could get behind. Dave wanted what he built with his personal ambition to affect personal change in someone else's life.

There's a lot of money and status that gets thrown around in the world of finance and politics, but Dave knew how to learn from every situation and appreciate everyone without losing himself. Most people can't wait to name-drop as well as talk about whom they know, what they've done, how important they are and what they've accomplished, But for as many bragging rights as he could claim, David Anderson understands that his faith, family and friends are what sustain him. He has never lost sight of what is real and important.

He is a true testament to the fact that what you are is defined by where you are going—not where you have come from. Life is not about what you do; it's about the person you become along the way. David has become a man that people can trust and a young leader that people can follow.

Introduction for Mark Nathan

David Anderson

Mark Nathan is one of a kind: a businessman, an innovator, and a leader. As a young adult, Mark was headed to the top of the theatre and film world. He paid his way through his university being an actor, finding it more practical to audition for paid professional roles than staying in the comfortable nest of his college campus. As he moved into directing and filmmaking, he found the venues for exposure at his school limiting, and started a successful film festival at twenty-one years old that had enough moving parts to make most professional event planners dizzy. To this day, he is constantly creating, innovating, and finding better ways to get things done. And when he was offered a professional opportunity that had the potential to catapult his acting career to celebrity status, he turned it down because he had a stronger vision for a more impactful career path.

I met Mark while he was working his day job and had dreams of being a big-time entrepreneur on the side. Someone said I had to hear him speak because he didn't just give talks, hearing Mark talk was an experience. I must admit, he didn't look that impressive. He wasn't a senior corporate executive, technology millionaire or Wall Street trader. He was a jeans and t-shirt guy who, in a one-on-one setting, was more likely to listen and ask questions than demand attention. However, I was astonished when he did finally open his mouth! He talked like someone at least fifteen years his senior, and had a gift for unveiling basic principles in the most fresh and dramatic ways, He didn't give superfluous information to sound fancy or intelligent. He just told the TRUTH! He is a powerful presence from stage, and I believe one of the great young communicators of this generation. He has spoken at sales events, leadership conferences and academic settings both in the U.S. and internationally, and to audiences of up to 10,000 people. As I built my own career, I watched him excel, marry

17

the girl of his dreams (Meredith) and continue down a path of success that was tangible and credible. And the success that Mark has created for himself is not a fundamentally self-serving one—rather, he has created it by solving problems in other people's lives, through servant leadership, and through relationship-building. There are some that have the privilege of having a small ripple-effect on the hundreds of thousands of people they'll never meet. Mark, on the other hand, has made a deep impact on the lives of those around him. His influence is etched deeply into those who have sought mentorship from him. Even in the darkest times of my own life, I have called on Mark to help me—and he demonstrated that same philosophy of service toward me. What seems "above and beyond" to most people is simply how Mark lives his life. Mark truly believes in the law of reciprocity. You can never give more to him than he will give to you. Mark is always serving, always giving, and always creating something to enrich people's lives. Truthfully, I probably would not be writing this book if it weren't for Mark. He was persistent in his vision to put something in the hands of the Millennial generation that could impact their lives for decades to come.

I have found that when people tell you who they are—that is, what they have accomplished, and what they can bring to the table—the reality is typically about seventy percent of what they make themselves out to be. He's not perfect, but Mark is one of the very few people I have met who is truly one-hundred percent of everything I continually hope him to be as a friend, business partner and young leader.

Most importantly, Mark truly adores his wife—a trait I admire in any man. And just as importantly, his wife truly adores him. As much as Mark has been admired from afar, those closest to him are the ones who admire him the most. I've seen a lot of people in my day: the rich, the powerful and the powerful rich. But, many of them don't have the wisdom and moral fortitude of Mark Nathan. You will gain great insights from his words.

What Happens When You Start With Bad Info
Mark Nathan

Find something you are passionate about, and you'll never feel like you're working a day in your life.

Follow your heart and passion. Money isn't everything.

The best people in every industry are the ones who are the most passionate about what they do.

To be truly successful in life, you must find your passion.

When you have discovered your true passion, every day is exciting.

Living with passion sounds like a really big deal...because it is.

We have heard everyone in our generation talk about passion: finding your passion, knowing your passion, living your passion — really pursuing life with all your heart and soul and utilizing your special talents and abilities in ways that add value to the world in a way that no one else can.

As I was growing up those types of statements inspired me! They sounded like truth. I felt that if I could figure out this passion thing, all the other pieces in my life would automatically come alive. Like a push-button start on a car, one simple move would spark life into every connected piece, giving each part the ability to function properly. I hoped that when I discovered my passion, I'd know what I should study in school and what kind of jobs to take. The moment I found my passion, I figured that the right people and relationships would show up in my life and I'd know exactly what to be doing with my time. And most importantly, when I unearthed my true calling, I would never again ask myself, "Isn't there more to life than this?"

As I grew up, I discovered good news and bad news:

The good news is that living a life of passion does actually exist. There are paths to pursue that make the days seem shorter and more fulfilling. There is a special and significant way that your strengths can add value to the world that is totally unique to you. You *should* live your life with all of your heart and all of your soul.

The bad news is that my whole concept of how to pursue a passionate life was completely backwards.

An Unofficial Survey of Passion

We call this an Unofficial Survey of Passion because the conversations that fed into this survey were not actually meant to be about the idea of passion at all. We spoke with thousands in our generation about their individual goals, dreams, and ambitions—and the word "passion" came up at least two-thirds of the time. Regardless of race, socio-economic background, education level or current career path, these conversations with 18–35 year olds had a recurring theme that was undeniable: these people all wanted to accomplish big things and live a life they were passionate about.

There was a sense that finding their passion wasn't just *a* piece to their puzzle, but *the* piece.

**The Unofficial Survey of Passion:
Living with passion is not only important,
but is vital to being fulfilled.**

What was interesting about these conversations was that although everyone agreed on the integral part that passion played in a successful life, very few people had any idea about how to get to the magical moment where they discovered what their passion might be. They had very clear thoughts on what living in that sweet spot would look like: money, promotion, lifestyle and respect. Unfortunately, there were very few definite ideas or plans on how to get there.

Here is a condensed recap of the most common sentiments expressed about passion:

When I find and follow my passion, people will really notice my gifts. Others will appreciate that I'm pursuing my calling and will want to help and open doors for me. It'd be great if someone spotted my gifts early on and helped me get ahead. If I'm following my passion, things will work out well and I will encounter very few problems.

When I find and follow my passion, I'll be pursuing something that is fun and makes me happy. I'll be living in my strengths and people will be supportive, so I probably won't struggle much. If I'm not loving it, it's probably a sign I'm doing the wrong things...because if I'm following my passion, there should be no pain.

When I find and follow my passion, I will recognize it immediately. I'll feel committed from the first moment—which is important, because I must be passionate about something before I commit fully.

When I find and follow my passion, I'll feel complete. I'll be happy knowing that I'm contributing in a unique way with my individual talents and abilities. I'll be content when I have found a way to maximize my gifts because finding happiness is about maximizing my dreams and goals.

When I find and follow my passion, every moment will be awesome. When I'm on the right path, I'll love every step and every day will be inspiring. It probably won't even feel like work! When I'm following my perfect path, I will be passionate about every step of the process.

These are all sentiments that we have felt or heard from others. These are all ideals many of us hope for and believe to be true.

Unfortunately, these statements are all delusions.

1° Off on Understanding Passion

Earlier we talked about the detriment of being 1° off. If you're traveling far distances, your plane being 1° off its flight plan could put you somewhere you never intended to be. The same is true in life, and it's definitely accurate when it came to my understanding of finding my passion.

I thought I was one of the lucky ones. I thought I had found my passion and my true calling early in life and I considered myself very fortunate. I got into acting after doing some video projects in high school, and I declared myself a theatre major in college with one show under my belt.

I took to it like a fish to water. I was talented at it. Even though I was brand new to the industry, I was being cast in what seemed like everything and getting a lot of positive feedback. I branched out into the professional Chicago scene pretty early and ended my college career having done more shows outside of school than in. I was signed with a few different agencies, consistently working, and paying my living expenses through college as an actor. I co-directed and produced some independent short films. In four years, there were five days that I was not rehearsing for a show or preparing for the next project. The time flew and it felt like I had really found my passion.

But even with some of that initial success, there were undeniably parts of me that did not feel completely right. I had other talents and abilities that I felt like I was under-utilizing or even ignoring completely. It felt like I wasn't in control of my life, like I was constantly waiting for someone else's approval so I could pay my bills. On top of that, it broke my heart that I couldn't help my family. At age nineteen, I would get calls from my parents asking me if I could help to pay the mortgage. I was so frustrated that I would turn it around on them and make them feel guilty for even asking. After all, weren't they supposed to be the ones supporting me when I needed help?

Yes, I was passionate about the work...but should I have been passionate about a life that didn't give me the control I wanted or the ability to care for my family?

Yes, I was proud of being part of a great project...but I definitely wasn't proud of myself when I would ignore my mom's phone calls when I knew they needed money.

Yes, I loved what I was doing...but how could I get excited about the idea of raising my future family always hoping for the next gig?

Finding vs. Creating

We believe that our generation is just 1° off about living a life of passion.

Finding your passion makes you passive. It keeps you waiting. It makes you a passenger in your own life.

Creating puts you in the driver's seat.

Finding your passion makes you passive.
Creating puts you in the driver's seat.

Most people have this idea that we should be trying to *find* our passion or *discover* our passion—like we're on some magical egg hunt for our perfect calling in life. What if we fine-tuned that notion just a bit? Instead of "finding our passion," what if we started *creating* a life we could be passionate about living?

Most people know the saying, "life is a journey." But do they live that way? Do they see their current situation as simply a chapter of a greater story that unfolds everyday? Do they see struggle as that which will unlock something amazing on the other side? Do they truly embrace the idea that this year is not actually about this year at all, but rather about laying the foundation for next year and the years to come?

Creating a life of passion means the job you have right now isn't just a line on your résumé. It's an experience and learning lesson that, if learned properly now, will play an irreplaceable role in your life years later in a completely different context. The opportunities that show up in your life now may be the way to develop skills and disciplines you'll come to rely on down the road.

Creating a life of passion means that you aren't the victim (or beneficiary) of the people in your life. They are there to teach you valuable lessons (good and bad) that will prepare you to unlock a new level of success in your life. There will be friends and partners who will add immeasurable value to your life, just as you will contribute to their lives—and there will be others who will teach you valuable lessons in what you *don't* want to emulate, and who you *don't* want to be.

Creating a life of passion means that you're in a real-life video game, developing skills and gathering experiences at every turn. The people you meet along the way will reveal their full purpose in your life when you least expect it. The relationships you develop now could play an irreplaceable role in what happens to you next month or ten years from now. The lessons you learn will unlock new levels of accomplishment.

But *how* do we create a life we're passionate about? Step by step, how does that *actually* happen? What does living a passionate life look like? How will we know if we're on the right track? Will there be fireworks or signs when we find it? If we screw up and make a wrong move, can we recover? So many of us know that we want to live a life full of passion, but we're completely clueless about where to begin.

We want answers. Consciously or unconsciously, we gather information to solve this problem. We see movies, Facebook posts and tweets, and we start piecing together an understanding of what a passionate life might look like. But are we looking for answers in all the wrong places?

The goal of this book is very simple: to clear up some misconceptions and delusions that we've found many have about living a life of passion. David and I struggled with the same confusion and learned the truth about passion through a lot of hard work, mentorship and falling on our faces. We see entirely too many in our generation stagnate in their lives, miss opportunities, and accomplish a fraction of what they are capable of—all because they started with the wrong info. Too many have wasted precious years because they began their journey misinformed.

The Delusions and Creating a Life of Passion

There are five delusions of passion we've seen stagnate the lives of hundreds of our peers, keeping them from living a life they are truly excited about. Let's clarify truth from misunderstanding.

After we've done that, we'll give you a few basic action steps that have helped Dave and I create lives that we are continually excited about.

If we can just get pointed in the right direction, our generation is going to be a force.

Part I:
The Delusions of Passion

Delusion #1:
Where There is Passion, There Is No Pain

David Anderson

The ultimate measure of a man is not where he stands in moments of comfort and convenience, but where he stands at times of challenge and controversy.

~ Martin Luther King, Jr.

When you think of a person like Martin Luther King, Jr., do you think of passion or pain? Many of us in the U.S. were taught his story of heroism, leadership, sacrifice and his fight for equality. We celebrate his birthday every year without fail and may even get a vacation day from work. We espouse his beliefs, morals, philosophies and words of wisdom. However, most citizens would never volunteer to go through the pain that Martin Luther King, Jr. endured. He was once stabbed by a lady in the chest for no reason, thrown into jail numerous times, rejected by the people he was trying to liberate, and was closely watched by the FBI because at the time he was considered a "trouble maker" and even a "terrorist." Sadly, King died at the young age of thirty-eight, but the autopsy report showed that his heart had aged to that of a sixty year-old.

Ironically, at the end of the twentieth century, Americans chose King as the second "Most Admired" person of the century. In 2006, Gallup released a study on King's likability while he was alive:

- In 1963, King had a 41% positive and a 37% negative rating.
- In 1964, he had a 43% positive and 39% negative rating.
- In 1965, his rating was 45% positive and 45% negative.

29

- In 1966 (the last Gallup measure of King), it was 32% positive and 63% negative.

Now, imagine if you walked down the street and out of every ten people, six of them hated you. That was King's reality. Yet, somehow all of that pain, hate and rejection produced one of the most passionate individuals America has ever known.

This is a truth about passion that is hard for us to grapple with. It seems counterintuitive that our path to passion would be riddled with pain. In fact, we have been taught to avoid pain: if it's painful, something must be wrong; if it's hurting or uncomfortable, just quit; if you'd rather not do the task, outsource it. Our aversion to pain may be the reason why we cherish this delusion and hold it so dear. We protect our decisions to give up on the challenges of life with the idea that if pain is present, perhaps it's the wrong path. But the truth is bittersweet: not only is living a passionate life going to *involve* pain, a truly passionate life is often *birthed from* pain.

A truly passionate life is often birthed from pain.

Learning through Personal Pain

Looking back at my own personal history, I see those inseparable friends, passion and pain, tap-dancing their way through my life. They've cemented my values and made me who I am today. Growing up, I faced certain challenges that were unusual for a teenage boy to have to deal with.

In addition to being a product of divorce, living below the poverty line and coming from "the wrong side of the tracks," my mother was schizophrenic. The responsibility fell to me to control our family finances, take care of my younger brother and sister and make sure we had food to eat. This was easier said than done. Like many schizophrenics, my mother bounc-ed back and forth between clarity and delusion, often being coherent. She struggled between a fear of losing control and a total inability to get basic things done. Though I had obtained power of attorney as our family decision maker, she would go behind my back to reclaim legal authority. And then she would forget to do basic things like apply for food stamps.

I remember one summer day when it was 105 degrees and there was no food left in our fridge. I was completely broke, and yet somehow I managed to scrounge together $25. The grocery store was over a mile away, and given the heat I decided to call a member of my family. This man was, in many ways, a father figure to me. He lived in a nearby neighborhood, and was doing very well by comparison. I had no intention of asking to borrow money, but I hoped he would lend me a car so that I could make the trip to the grocery store and back. After all, he had four of them. I dialed the number and made my request. He responded:

"David, you know I don't loan out my cars. You're just going to have to figure out another way."

As I walked to that grocery store, sweat dripping all down my body—and as I walked back carrying four heavy bags of whatever $25 could buy for my mother, brother and sister to eat—a lot of thoughts ran through my mind:

Why did God allow my mom to become schizophrenic?

Why would family refuse to help family when they're in need?

Why are we living in a situation where we can barely afford groceries?

Would I even have these problems if my mom and dad had stayed together?

Is this the life that I am destined to live? If so, it's horrible!

By the time I returned home, I was exhausted, dehydrated and covered in sweat. I was met by my mother, who looked through the groceries and saw that I had purchased turkey bacon instead of pork bacon. This triggered one of her episodes; she went ballistic and tore through the kitchen, cursing at me for my mistake.

I know there are more dramatic injustices in the world, and even in comparison to my own teenage years it was a pretty tame, mundane moment. After all, I'd been surrounded by and involved in neighborhood gangs as a teenager. I'd been introduced to drug dealing at a very young age and I'd wanted to start my own drug-distribution market on the streets. I'd only recently given up that trade after a life-altering spiritual encounter. But at that moment, I'd had it. I completely broke down and wanted to give up. I hid myself in an upstairs room and sobbed. Fortunately, I also called my pastor, Albert Toledo of the Chicago Tabernacle. I'll never forget the words he spoke to me:

"David, I don't know why God is allowing you to go through this, but it is going to make you more of a man than anything you've ever known."

Those words were exactly what I needed to hear; it was one of those defining moments in my life. I, David Anderson, covered in tears and sweat, back from a mission to bring chicken and turkey bacon into my family's kitchen, discovered a passion for the responsibility of manhood. I didn't know why some people wouldn't take ownership of the well-being of those who were depending on them, or why some wouldn't even take ownership of themselves. But in that moment, I swore that I would never be one of those people. The pain of *not* having what so many children take for granted—someone who will take responsibility for them —gave me a more intense passion for being a person who would take responsibility.

The intense pursuit of responsibility guided so many of the decisions in my life that followed. It was why I postponed going to school, and eventually why I went. It was why I sought greater opportunities to earn income for my family. It was why I briefly entered the political arena, and why I started my own business. It's why I got married, and why I've stayed married even when times have been tough.

A few years after this incident, I went to work for a man named Ernest. He had gone to Harvard Law and was starting up his own law practice. Though I knew nothing of law or of his world in general, I'd always had an entrepreneurial spirit; in fact, prior to cleaning up my life, I'd developed a comprehensive business plan for my drug-running endeavors.

I channeled these instincts into Ernest's practice, and found I took naturally to helping him build and run his firm. I spent two and a half years helping him with his operation, and learned from him the culture and manners of the business world. Though I knew I didn't have a future in law, I saw the potential for me to build a successful career path for myself—as I'd helped Ernest do for himself.

Getting to Wall Street

In 2009, I decided I was going to get on Wall Street. I enrolled at Chicago State University. I took courses in finance and dedicated myself entirely to my studies. I had a 4.0 and was at the top of my class. After a period of proving myself, I went to the Career Development Office to speak with the director. This man had a long and rich career, having worked at notable universities such as Notre Dame, Rochester, and Duke prior to CSU. I knew he had information that most didn't have; information that could help me advance my career. After a firm hand shake, I looked him in the eye and told him with all the confidence I could muster that my goal was to go to Wall Street and work for one of the top financial firms. He looked blankly at me, and then burst into laughter.

I paused, and dumbly asked "Why are you laughing?"

He paused, catching his breath. "David...you picked the wrong school."

I knew he was telling the truth. CSU certainly wasn't paying him to tell me that. And I was furious. After all my years in business, my time in class and studying, after everything I'd sacrificed even to be able to go to school, the Director of CSU's Career Development Program was telling me that I'd picked a dead end— that I needed to give up, or find a new dream. My anger and indignation escalated, until suddenly a solution popped into my brain:

If CSU was the *wrong* school, I'd go to the career fairs at all the *right* schools.

Off I went after classes and on weekends to every recruiting event I caught wind of at the University of Chicago and Northwestern. Determined not to lie, when I was asked about my studies I found ways to dodge questions and answer in vague terms. I became a regular, to the point where people knew me and assumed I must belong. Finally an opportunity hit, and I was granted an interview for a summer position with Goldman Sachs.

The interview process was a multi-step, grueling ordeal, and one where I could no longer hide my alma mater. And the culture at Goldman Sachs was not one of softness and niceties:

"What was your GPA at school? 4.0? Impressive. Where did you go? Chicago State University? What the *%#& is Chicago State University? Well...nobody cares about your 4.0."

I'd worked so hard to achieve everything I had done up to that point. No one there knew me. They didn't know about my schizophrenic mom. They didn't know I'd left a lifestyle of drug dealing and associations with gang members. They didn't know the pain of the decision to even go to school, because of my concern for leaving my little brother and sister alone with my mother. How dare they belittle me and all my efforts? All that rejection and ridicule welled up inside me, but out of it grew a passion to be proud of whom I was, and everything that I'd accomplished up to that point:

"I'm Chicago State University, and I'm gonna put it on the map. You got a problem with that?"

I finally made it to the last interview for the position, and was flown out to New York. The interview was an all-day process. Candidates were flown in from all over the U.S., and all the interviewees were herded into one room to wait their turn. I looked around at my fellow applicants and saw how utterly out of place I was. Every one of these students seemed to have been groomed their entire lives for this moment. These people came from better universities than I did and had better backgrounds than I had. They were better dressed than I was. But through the rough-and-tumble culture of Goldman Sachs I'd grown accustomed to the pain of not fitting in, and I'd developed a passion for being honest about whom I was and what made me ME.

My name was called, and I entered the interview room.

"So, why do you want to work at Goldman Sachs," the interviewer asked. I gave him my pitch, answered his questions, and told him about my experience. Finally I said:

"Look, let me be honest with you. You're gonna talk to a lot of smart people today, and they're all going to be incredible. I'm probably the least likely person to be in here, as you know because you've looked at my resume. So, you also know what I've had to do even to get to this table. And I don't think there's anybody else you're going to interview today that wants this more than I do."

He paused, sat back in chair, and looked at me. "I believe you." I beat out all the rest of the applicants and got the position for the Investment Banking Summer in New York. After that summer, they called on me to work in their Chicago office. And my career in finance was launched.

1° Off: Pain Is Part of Pursuing Passion

What if I'd shied away from the discomfort of being around hard people? What if I'd quit because it just didn't feel good to get ridiculed? What if I'd felt insecure and out of place and decided I must not be on the right path? So many people quit on their dreams, goals and plans because of the painful process to the finish line. But this philosophy isn't consistent with success at all. Pain is part of the process, and anyone who has achieved high levels of success will tell you so. Why? Because pain is what guards the extraordinary. The pain is what turns most people away, and rewards the persistent people with accomplishment.

Have you ever seen the way a mother cherishes and bonds with her child? The idea that living a life of passion is not painful is a delusion. Mothers love their children in a way that fathers can only envy. It's true that both men and women release the bonding hormones of oxytocin and epinephrine. However, I guarantee that if men went through the pain of childbirth, they would have a different appreciation for the reward at the end of process. There is simply a different level of love that a mother has for her newborn child because she physically went through the pain of pregnancy and labor.

Pain is what guards the extraordinary.

We look at people with tremendous physiques and wonder how they have stayed in shape. Well, they probably go through the pain of working out and eating the right foods every day. I envy them, because I love cheesecake and apple pie too much! The pain in your body from a hard workout is literally your muscles being ripped and torn apart, which enables them to rebuild even stronger.

What about entrepreneurs who have built very successful businesses from scratch and are now worth millions of dollars? They get to spend their time the way they want, travel when they want and spend time with their family when they want. Best of all, they get to avoid rush-hour traffic! However, being a successful entrepreneur is probably one of the hardest job titles in the world. You constantly face rejection, have to motivate and organize people, be disliked, take risks with your own money, and sacrifice paychecks. An entrepreneur friend of mine, Ernest, decided he'd either have to "go through the pain of hoping for a paycheck or the pain of creating my own. No matter which way I choose, pain is on the other side."

Being a mom, being passionate about fitness, pursuing entrepreneurship, and Martin Luther King, Jr.—all of these things have pain in common. No matter how deeply passionate you are, there will be moments where you are hurting physically, mentally and/or emotionally.

Of course, I'm not suggesting you seek out pain because you believe it will help you accelerate in life. As you continue down the path towards passion, you won't need to seek out pain and discomfort—pain and discomfort will find you as you take on new challenges.

Don't avoid pain, embrace it. Embracing the hurt is what creates a deeper level of respect and connection. Pain is the process of true passion being born.

Chapter Review

Delusion: If I'm struggling or hurting, I must be on the wrong path.

Reality: Growing pains are part of the process if you want to do something amazing.

37

Delusion #2:
Where There is Passion, There Are No Problems
Mark Nathan

I believe there are signs from the universe to let us know that we're on the right track. Of course, most people think that I'm referring to the "signs" you see in the movies. That if something is meant to be, a mysterious connection will be made and all the stars will align. Or perhaps some wise, old person will give us a crucial piece of advice that will lead us to our destiny. Or maybe our quirky best friend will remind us of something that happened in our childhood that confirms everything we're doing with our life right now.

Whether it's from too many romantic comedies or inspirational movie montages, most of us have believed that when we find our true calling (in life or in love), we'll get warm-and-fuzzy feelings, things will magically start to come together and problems will most certainly work themselves out. As long as we're passionate about what we're doing, good will prevail and we will float above all resistance on the wings of inspiration...

We haven't reconciled the fact that our unshakable faith in the future doesn't mean there won't be stormy seas along the way.

Problems are Part of the Story

In his book, *Good to Great*, Jim Collins coins the term "The Stockdale Paradox," based on Admiral James Stockdale, a POW who was imprisoned for eight years during the Vietnam War. Collins notes that Stockdale found an unwavering faith that he and the rest of the POW's would get through their current situation. But it wasn't simple optimism. In fact, Stockdale said that pure optimism was a virtual death sentence, because the optimists would die of a broken heart.

What caught the attention of Collins was how Stockdale balanced his faith in a positive outcome with the brutal reality of his current situation. He was, after all, in a POW camp where he was being tortured and forced into isolation. Understanding fully the grimness of his situation, he created systems to help him and the other POW's deal with their circumstances and better handle the pain. He created a makeshift morse code that enabled the prisoners to communicate with each other, thereby diminishing the intensity of the isolation. He also knew that during torture, it wasn't a question of if you were going to break and reveal information, but rather of when you would break and how much information would you reveal. He created a structure for the prisoners detailing what types of information to give at certain minute markers during the torture sessions. This allowed the prisoners to focus on a short term goal and reveal non-pertinent information, rather than fully breaking and telling it all. He dealt head-on with the problems at-hand while keeping an eye on the vision of freedom.

Collins related the wisdom and experience of Admiral Stockdale to how companies deal with their goals in a constantly changing business environment. Great companies create a vision for the future, all the while acknowledging with brutal honesty the company's current shortcomings. If you apply those same principles to personal development, you have the story of Peter Daniels, Australian billionaire.

I first met Mr. Daniels during his last tour through the US, at a conference being held at Family Harvest Church. This is where I first started to learn his story.

Peter began his young adult life as an illiterate bricklayer. The future didn't look particularly bright, but in his mid-twenties he had a life-changing experience with God and realized that he was made for more. However, just because he _knew_ he was made for more didn't mean he was properly _equipped_ for more. He had a passion to prosper, to be a testimony to the greatness of God and to impact others—but the brutal reality was that he worked in a trade where he had limited direct impact on other people's lives. He had never achieved high levels of academic success. He couldn't even read. So he dealt with the hard facts of his situation.

As an adult, he met with a member of his church who was willing to offer his tutelage, and Peter learned to read, one week at a time. He transitioned into a sales role, which required learning a whole different skill set (not to mention mental toughness). Over the years, there were a number of failed businesses, critics, and national and global issues he had to deal with, but he just dealt with them one at a time. Peter had a passion to live a Godly life and positively impact the world, but in the pursuit of that he had to confront the brutal facts of being an illiterate bricklayer. Decades later, he has read over a thousand autobiographies, has become a real-estate mogul and investment genius, and has influenced millions of people worldwide.

If you want to pursue greatness and a life of passion, don't ignore the brutal fact that there are issues to deal with. The Stockdale Paradox, applied to your personal development, means that if you're going to achieve greatness, you need both a driving vision for your future (your passion) and an honest assessment of your shortcomings (your problems).

Pursuing your passion and overcoming your problems are inextricably tied together.

Pursuing your passion and overcoming your problems are inextricably tied together.

The Role of Problems

There is a difference between the facts of your life and the problems in your life (although in many cases they'll revolve around the same thing!).

It's a fact that my family did not have much money when I was growing up, but that fact became a problem when I wanted to start making movies and we couldn't afford a camera.

It was a fact that I had a tendency to mumble when I spoke, but that fact became a problem when I wanted to be a leader, which requires communication skills.

It was a fact that I was a little bit lazy, but that fact became a problem when I wanted to be an entrepreneur.

Facts become problems when they're cramping your style. When the facts impede your progress in life, they become problems that need to be dealt with.

Our problems can originate from a number of different places. Some of our problems come from our own personal challenges, like personality issues or bad habits. Some are environmental, like living in a dangerous neighborhood or having limited exposure to different types of people growing up. Some problems are caused by outside circumstances, like other people or unfamiliar situations. Some problems come from you being a victim, while others may be your own fault. In any case, you're required to take responsibility for all of them if you are going to make progress finding your passion.

Obviously, life would be easier if we didn't have any problems to deal with. Having an unobstructed road to all of life's rewards would be great! But the problems we think are cramping our style may actually have a much more important role in our future than we realize.

Problems identify weaknesses that will stop you from being amazing.

Nature gives us a great understanding of this principle when we watch the simple brilliance of a caterpillar emerging from its cocoon. The newly formed butterfly is battling with the fact that it's inside of its silk shell. It wants to be outside so it can start to fly. But what the butterfly doesn't know is that the problem it's facing is actually what will give it the strength to accomplish the end goal! The struggle to get out of the cocoon is the time the butterfly develops the wing strength it needs to take flight. If it's not strong enough to break out of its cocoon, it's not strong enough to fly.

Knowing this, would you want to help the butterfly get out of its cocoon? If you saw it struggling, would you assist it and cut the slit open to speed things up? In helping the butterfly avoid its "problems," you would essentially sentence it to death.

Overcoming your "problems" will actually provide you with the qualities you'll need to live the life you are meant to live. What you find in any problem isn't a struggle—it's the strength to move on.

Problems identify weaknesses that will stop you from being amazing. If you agree that all of us have natural strengths that can accelerate us to glory, it stands to reason that we all have natural weaknesses that will keep us from attaining glory. Your problems are not a big deal if you understand what they are. They are simply revealing areas that need to be dealt with in order for you to be fully awesome.

What you find in any problem isn't a struggle —it's the strength to move on.

The Role of Passion

Now that we've acknowledged that everyone knows they have problems, it begs the question: why don't people do something about it?

One farmer sees his friend's dog lying down on a broken porch. He remarks, "That old dog is lying on a nail. Why doesn't he move?" The friend answers, "Well, I guess it just doesn't hurt bad enough."

Sometimes in life, it's easier to just not move. It's easier to complain and whine about the problems in life: to blame your parents for not having the money to provide more opportunities, to blame your coach for not giving you a fair shot—and above all else, to find a scapegoat for why life isn't turning out like you wanted. It's more comfortable to make excuses than to deal with the problems we know are waiting for us just around the corner.

That's where passion comes in! Your passions and desires in life will be the spark that causes you to get off that nail. Your passion will also help you weather the storms. I remember in drivers ed class, they taught us to "aim high in steering," because the farther down the road you focus, the less jerky your driving will be and the smoother all the twists and turns become. Your passion will give you a vision for the future and, through that, a willingness to embrace your problems.

Passion will help you navigate the storm...but no one ever said anything about avoiding the storm.

Passion will help you navigate the storm, but no one said anything about avoiding the storm.

Overcoming Your Problems Prepares You

I had a few personal habits that became problems for me as I wanted to level-up in my life. Here are just a few issues that I struggled with:

I had become entitled. In school, I got used to teachers giving out a syllabus and telling you exactly how to get an "A" in the class. In college, I studied both theatre and education, and both departments had a lot to offer. The education department already had after-school programs running at nearby schools, so I had my pick of opportunities that worked best for my schedule. As a theatre major, eight productions throughout the year provided plenty of opportunity to develop my craft right there at school. There was constantly someone laying out a perfect path and providing me with opportunities...but when I decided to throw my hat into the professional-theatre ring, no one brought me anything. I had gotten used to others telling me or giving me exactly what I needed to get to the next level.

No one likes to be called entitled (me, especially), but if you've ever waited for someone to do or provide something for you that you can do for yourself, that's being entitled. As a result, I had to provide and create opportunities for myself. I learned to seek out auditions instead of waiting for them. I stayed on top of the trade papers, searched online, and actively sent out my headshots and resumes weekly. When I got auditions, I took trains, buses, bikes, and even flew across the country just to get my foot in the door. I began to seek out the best agents and not just sit by the phone hoping for a call.

Another major interest of mine was directing and producing. After completing my first independent short film, my co-creator Jon and I began submitting our film-baby to student film festivals across the country. However, after going through this process several times, it occurred to me that rather than wait to see in what remote place the film would be aired, I should create my own film festival locally in Chicago. In doing this, I could not only feature my own project, but also provide exposure for other local student films as well. It had become second nature at that point to create opportunities instead of waiting for them, so off I went on this new adventure.

Though the habit of creating opportunities was already well-formed in me, I also had to acknowledge that I had no idea what I was doing. As such, the first thing I went in search of was a little mentorship. I arranged an interview with the festival director of the Chicago International Film Festival, so I could pick her brain about how to fund, advertise and orchestrate an event like this.

Next, I needed a location and sponsors. And to get either, you have to convince companies that their partnership with you will yield a return for them. I created a formal presentation projecting potential sponsors, brand advertising and expected numbers of attendees (and by expected, I really meant hoped for!). Meanwhile, we advertised all around Chicagoland for submissions to our festival. I targeted seven different schools in the area and obtained a student contact at each location, chatted with professors, and papered the campuses with flyers.

Finally, I had to create a marketing buzz around our event to make sure seats would be filled and all of these films would get the exposure they needed.

This was largely before social media, and we didn't have a marketing budget to speak of, so we had to get a little creative. Since we picked films from each of the seven different colleges, we capitalized on school pride and created an unofficial campus competition to see which school would represent the strongest. By the time it was all said and done, the Chicago Collegiate Film Festival had over fifty submissions, nine sponsors, and over 300 audience members in attendance. I was twenty-one years old at the time, and from the inception of the idea to its fruition, only three months had passed.

Please don't misunderstand me. I'm not suggesting I executed this process perfectly, or that I wouldn't improve aspects of this event if I were to do it again. But I would never have even attempted such a project if I hadn't learned from my "problems." In those years of overcoming my entitlement, I had actually developed the skills that would later serve me as an entrepreneur.

Another major hurdle that I needed to overcome was disorganization. My schedule was a train wreck. I was forgetful. I was always running late. When I started building my online retail business, I had a deeply ingrained habit of flying by the seat of my pants and "winging it." As such, my lack of accountability and inability to be punctual cost me opportunities. Often, I showed up to find a frustrated prospect who was no longer excited about working with me. Of course, I always had a perfectly rationalized excuse for my shortcomings, whether it was traffic, the weather or my job. But how many times could I blame traffic before I just accepted that tardiness was a personal problem that needed to be dealt with? It's hard to trust someone who is always making excuses. So I had to learn to own my failures whenever I screwed up, and to lead myself through them.

To deal with my disorganized nature, I figured out systems that kept me more structured and on top of my game. First and foremost, I bought a PAPER calendar. This may sound really archaic, but for me it was a revelation. Today a lot of people keep their calendar on their smart phone; this may be a fine way to write down appointments, but for me it was a terrible way to plan my time. Looking at my appointments on paper got me thinking about when I needed to leave for them. It also got me keeping a written to-do list, and allowed me to put that list into blocks of time (which meant my to-do's actually got done!).

I decided to end my love affair with the snooze button in favor of having a morning routine. I set my alarm across the room so that I'd have to get out of bed in order to turn it off (since I was already a champ at hitting snooze without actually waking up). I trained myself to get out of bed, turn off my alarm, and keep walking into the shower all before my brain had actually "turned on." By the time the water hit me, I was awake and able to get a good start to my day.

I needed these new habits ingrained in me, since I knew that I wouldn't excel at my job *and* be able to move my online business forward if I didn't up my game. But it couldn't stop there. I needed a real personal-growth plan, in addition to my action plan, so that I could build me while I was building my business. But where would I find time for a personal growth plan *and* a business plan when I already worked/commuted for fifty hours a week?

With my new time-management systems in place, I actually found this process surprisingly simple. I made my non-productive time productive by keeping success-oriented CD's in my car and listening to them on my commute to work each day. I kept a book at my desk and read for at least fifteen minutes on my lunch break. I made the commitment to make at least one business call while at work (either at lunch or on my afternoon break), so that I would be able to do something for my business during the work day.

Of course this didn't all happen overnight. I took it one week at a time, and just tried to be better during the current week than I was the previous one. But over time, sticking with these systems and habits paid off. Years later, my wife and I have had the privilege of leading and influencing hundreds. We've created systems and apps that are utilized by people across the country, and maximizing personal potential is the number-one topic about which we are asked to share when we speak publicly.

Even though you're passionate about something, there is still a lot of work to be done.

1° Off: Problems Prepare You

What are the "problems" that you need to overcome to get to the next level?

Perhaps you're not effective at communicating with people? If that's your problem, tackle it ASAP because effectively working with people is important no matter what industry you're in.

Maybe you're a little lazier than you'd like to be, or you've become a champion procrastinator? If that is your problem, learn to work hard and plan your time more effectively.

Perhaps you've become a little too sensitive and hung up on other people's opinions? If that's a problem, overcome your approval addiction or you won't break out of the norm and have above-average results.

When you embrace your problems, you embrace the future that awaits you when you overcome them.

Remember the Stockdale Paradox from earlier: keep a positive vision of the future while dealing with the brutal facts of today. Take a really honest look at what you need to deal with right now, so that you can continue to shape the future you want.

There are certain things to learn before you can move on to the next level in anything. In video games (which I have played a lot), you learn one skill at a time, collect one item at a time, master one weapon at a time. What you learn in Level 2 equips you for Level 3. What you learn in Level 3 will need to become second nature by Level 7. By Level 11, you're really having fun because you're simply good at everything!

In life, you can't have Level 11 rewards if you can't get past your Level 2 problems! (We'll chat in lots of detail about "Leveling-Up" in life in a later chapter.)

That's why you shouldn't avoid problems; you should embrace them. When you learn to embrace the problems in front of you, you also embrace the future that awaits you. When you begin to develop a track record of overcoming struggle, it stops being a question of *if* you will win, but rather how big will you win.

Chapter Review

Delusion: If I'm on the right path, it should be easy to move forward.

Reality: If you're on the right path, problems are opportunities that allow you to level up.

49

Delusion #3:
Passion Precedes Total Commitment

Mark Nathan

I'm always trying to figure out the formula for success. I know it's not an exact science, but I can't help but hear stories of highly accomplished people and try to pick out common themes. Across different industries and personalities, what are the similar components to achieving success, and is there a general process that we could follow to achieve similar results?

In story after story, I've noticed a few common themes:

Passion: So many people talk about passion that we have inextricably tied passion and success together (hence the inspiration for this book). Successful people are so fired up and consumed by what they're accomplishing, it's tough not to be inspired.

Engagement: Everyone gets started somewhere, and it's typically not at "sold out." Before anyone could succeed at a high level, they went through a humbling season of knowing nothing, being the new kid on the block, and may have even been unsure if they chose the right industry.

Commitment: Being "sold out" or "all-in" is the best way to describe it. Successful people have a complete dedication to understanding their industry and the intricacies of what they do. Their level of focus and work ethic freaks out the normal people.

Achievement: Similar to success, this is obviously the end goal. Accomplish big things, contribute to society, make an impact and provide for your family—that's what life is all about! If we can accomplish those things, we have taken a big step toward personal fulfillment.

Progression Toward Success

Obviously there are many more components to success—but from a view of ten thousand feet, here's how I understood the four components listed above. In story after story, I assembled what I believed to be the formula for success:

PASSION   ENGAGEMENT   COMMITMENT   ACHIEVEMENT

EQUALS

SUCCESS

*This is definitely not true…*but I thought it was.

But before we dive into the role of passion in this progression, let's start with the areas most everyone can agree on.

ENGAGEMENT   COMMITMENT

Engagement Precedes Commitment

Commitment is a progressive thing. I think everyone can understand and get behind this concept. You don't get sold out to something on day one. Your engagement and commitment grow day by day and week by week.

If you have friends who do fantasy football, you've seen this lived out right in front of you. Take a hometown fan that likes to watch his team every week. Then introduce him to fantasy football, where you attach points to different aspects of the game, add in the ability to make his own dream team, and you've just electrified his game-watching experience! He really enjoys this added dimension to the game and decides to join a league.

The next season he rejoins the same league, and since he's learned the ropes, he decides to add a few more. He continues to have more fun and the following season he's upped his commitment to five leagues and decides to take a stab at running a small fantasy league of his own. Before you know it, he's a member of ten leagues and is running two of them. This football fan that used to enjoy watching his hometown team once a week now spends his entire weekend flipping between multiple games on TV, has two more games pulled up on his laptop, and his free time is now fully consumed by organizing players for his dozen or more leagues. Now that's commitment!

Another great example is college students, who are some of the most committed people you will ever meet, in my opinion. They are committed to their school, their grades, their social life and their teams. But not all colleges are equal in that regard. I don't have any in-depth, Malcolm Gladwell-like studies on the subject, but for the last decade, I have talked to hundreds of college students from dozens of schools. Those who were the most passionate about their school were always the ones who were the most involved.

Also, from what I've seen, the major universities (those with huge sports programs, Ivy League schools, etc.) are typically the ones that best create an environment of involvement, and therefore have the most committed alumni. It seems that the bigger the school is, the more opportunities there are for students to get involved. There are more sports teams playing more games, student associations for every type of student from every type of background, more alma-mater-branded sweatshirts, mascot-laden t-shirts, and even school-pride sweatpants for wearing to bed (and then to class the next day!). Many large universities also have an abundance of dorms and student housing, so students live on the campus and spend more time being immersed in the environment. The more immersed students are in the environment, the more interest they develop in becoming engaged. And ultimately, commitment evolves from this continual engagement.

I remember this same principle playing out shortly after my wife and I got married. We wanted to find a church to call home, and so we started attending and vetting different services on our free weekends. There were a handful of things that were very important to us: what the church believed, how we connected to the community and how we saw the congregation living out their faith. Finally we went to a church where the message was everything we had hoped for. The excitement, the foundation, the people, their commitment to their faith, their goals as an organization—everything seemed to line up that first week we went. Do you think that we went to the pastor afterward and said, "We'd like to be members and you can plan to see us every Sunday for the rest of our lives!"?

Of course not. We were very encouraged by what we heard and experienced...and we were committed enough to come back the next week. Then the following week came and we were excited to come back once more. Then we grabbed lunch with one of the couples in leadership there and asked some questions. And then we were back the next week. After a couple of months of continually getting more engaged, we were excited and committed members of the church, and we've been there for years.

> ## Commitment is a progressive thing; don't be afraid to start somewhere and just get involved.

Never forget that commitment is a progressive thing. Whether you're trying a new sport or activity, exploring a new business opportunity, or developing a new friendship or partnership, don't be afraid to start somewhere and just get involved. There will undoubtedly be many factors to consider as you begin, but don't get buried in the "what if" scenarios. For every uncertainty you can foresee, there are dozens of exciting possibilities that you don't even know to consider!

Take it one step at a time: evaluate your decision based on what you're looking for long-term, get started, and let your commitment grow in incremental steps.

COMMITMENT   ACHIEVEMENT

Commitment Produces Achievement

Real achievement and commitment always go hand in hand. You would be hard-pressed to find accomplished experts in any field who didn't first have a very vigorous schedule as they mastered their industry.

My senior-year high-school English teacher, Mr. White, told a story of hearing an internationally renowned violinist in concert. Afterwards, he was at a reception with the violinist and heard an impressed fan casually say, "You are such an amazing musician. I would give my life to play that well." The musician responded "I have already given my life to play this well."

You hear about the long nights that entrepreneurs put in to build their business, or the rigorous trainings that athletes endure. At the checkout counter of life, success is never on sale. You must always pay full price.

At the checkout counter of life, success is never on sale. You must always pay full price.

It's also worth taking a minute to talk about achieving success that's not at a pro-status, world-domination level. What if you're just looking to get a promotion? What if you're looking to get noticed? What if you just want to get to the next level?

I recently chatted with a young man who was wrapping up the summer between his sophomore and junior year of college. He was working at a shoe store and explained to me how this was the LAST summer he was going to work minimum wage. He said he felt like it was an insult to make that little and that if the store respected his ability, they'd pay him more.

But though he expected to be paid more, he wasn't actively doing more. Everyone understands when you move up the ladder at a company, you make more money. So if this guy truly wanted to make more, he needed to start doing things that would get him promoted. If he became a supervisor or assistant manager, his problems of not making enough and not feeling respected would be solved! What if instead of focusing on not being paid enough, he focused on how to grow his skill-set, add more value—and then move up the ladder?

How fast do you think he would have gotten noticed if he had started taking on more responsibility? Doing more than what he was asked before he was asked to do it? Helping out his co-workers as they needed help? Taking care of the appearance of the store so that every customer that walked in would have a first-class experience? What if he committed to the store like he was already an assistant manager...how fast would he have moved up? Maybe not in two weeks, but certainly in time he would have seen the results he desired!

Are there ways that you can perform at the next level so that you can reach the next level of success? If world-class success takes world-class commitment, then surely next-level success requires next-level commitment. Increased commitment always comes before increased success.

Increased commitment always comes before increased success.

Where Does Passion Fit In?

I believed that this whole process from engagement to success started with passion. To me, that was a no-brainer. Why would I even want to get involved in something that I wasn't excited about? You only live once (YOLO), so why spend time doing stuff that isn't exciting? If I wasn't feeling it...it was automatically a no-go. After all, with so many exciting options in the world, who has time to spend doing things that aren't awesome?

Furthermore, if success really required all of that work, how could I get through it without passion? How could I get over that initial bump of discomfort and extra work if I wasn't passionate from the start?

So before I would do anything, one of my decision filters was, "Am I truly passionate about this project? Can I really get behind this with everything I've got?"

In this paradigm, passion was both the foundation and the catalyst for success.

My Belief:

Why Starting with Passion Presents a Problem

The problem with letting our passion dictate what we do is that we often mistake our passion for our feelings. It's an understandable mistake. I feel very deeply for my family and will passionately protect them. I have very strong feelings about respecting other people, so when people are being disrespected, I get pretty fired up.

If things I feel deeply about produce passion, then if I'm passionate about something, it should produce a lot of deep feelings...right?

Now, you probably didn't sit down and have a formal chat with yourself about that line of thinking. And yet everyday people let their feelings be the litmus test for their actions. In fact, I believe the average person makes a large majority of their decisions based on feelings alone.

People want to lose weight, but they don't feel like going to the gym—they really just want to eat dessert. Thousands of students study through the night because they didn't feel like studying earlier in the week.

Hundreds of thousands of Americans struggle with their bills because they felt like eating out and chasing recreation a few too many times. People have things they're trying to accomplish, but too often they don't make progress because they let their emotions run their life.

When You Follow Your Feelings

My friend Greg describes feelings as schizophrenic. I heard him tell a story once about being on a drive with his beautiful wife and five kids. Staring out over the gorgeous landscape and surrounded by the family he loved, he felt very happy and at peace. A moment later he was cut off by another driver, and instantly Greg's feelings went from contentment to rage. Like any man with a competitive edge, he sped up and started to tailgate the car in front of him. However, as a successful business owner in the community, his public image suddenly dawned on him! As he chased down this person at eighty-five miles an hour, Greg wondered if perhaps this person was someone who might recognize him. His dominant feeling went from anger to embarrassment. Then the adrenaline passed, and he remembered he had his family in the car! His feelings went from embarrassment to remorse. Next, one of his kids punched the other in the face...and on and on it goes. This emotional rollercoaster occurred for Greg over just a ninety-second span!

Feelings don't care about you or your future. They don't filter through a brain cell or have a plan. They just happen. They can be influenced by chemicals firing in your brain, hormones in your body and even indigestion. If you make decisions based on just feelings, life will never give you the kind of results you want—because feelings are transient by nature and highly reactive, and nothing is smooth sailing all of the time.

If you let feelings run your life, you won't have a long-lasting relationship, because the emotion of love comes and goes.

If you let feelings run your life, you'll leave your kids every time they're being difficult.

If you let feelings run your life, you will fail in business, because success takes work and courage.

At some point, you won't feel like saying sorry to your spouse, changing a diaper, or making a phone call—so if you just follow your feelings, you are headed for disaster.

And if you can't trust your feelings to get you through the day, how much worse will it be if you're trying to make them the foundation for your life-long pursuit of success?

Feeling passion for something is not at all the same as *living* with passion. The feeling of passion is just as unreliable and fleeting as any other feeling in your life. Like we've said already, feelings don't care about you or your future.

DON'T FORGET

You may feel excited, nervous or completely indifferent before something new in your life, but just as those feelings are temporary, feeling passionate about a project is temporary as well.

Feeling passionate is not a reliable litmus test for whether you should take the next steps in your life. Living with the delusion that you must feel passionate before you engage, commit and achieve big things is too often a formula for failure!

When Passion Really Shows Up

The reason most people spend a long, long time trying to figure out what they're passionate about is that they think passion is what starts it all. It's like they've put their life on pause until they can figure out their passion—then, and only then, can they finally start living.

The truth is that the passion you're looking for—the passion that inspires people, makes your family proud, and leaves this world a better place—happens at the end. Not at the end of life, but at the end of a process. That's not to say you won't experience passion along the way,

59

but don't be surprised if it's fleeting, and certainly don't rely on it to get you to where you want to be.

Getting started and becoming involved doesn't require passion. Moving from engagement to commitment doesn't require passion. Staying committed until you start accomplishing small goals doesn't require passion.

After you've achieved a little success, you can look back and identify the things that you connected with the most. You can see what you really loved doing and what moved you. The passion you so desperately want to find is actually something you unlock and create on your way to your next success.

The truth:

ENGAGEMENT COMMITMENT ACHIEVEMENT PASSION

EQUALS

SUCCESS

In Action

My brother is a Catholic Priest. Father Matt, or Father-Brother Matt as I call him, is a pretty awesome dude. He's very likely the only breakdancing, Spanish-speaking, Asian priest out there. However, he didn't start out by committing to being a dancer, speaking Spanish, or being a priest! In fact, he wasn't excited about ANY of those things ten years ago while he was still in college

Like many, he started his young-adult life trying to figure out what he was passionate about. Like many Asians, he thought his calling was to help people by being a doctor, so he went pre-med during his undergrad. But when he got involved in different programs that gave him exposure to the field, he realized it was not the path for him. Then he thought his path might be medical research, so he committed to it and switched his major to microbiology. After an internship that got him involved in the day-to-day routine of medical research, he knew that was also not for him. At this point, he was already done with undergrad, so he went on to get his Master's in Education. He thought he might be passionate about teaching: he was good at it, he liked kids, and it generally sounded like a good fit. But during grad school, a funny thing happened.

Matt's calling to the priesthood didn't at all follow his above "pattern." One day at mass, someone said, "Maybe you know you're called to be a priest, but most don't. Unless you know you're definitely NOT called to be a priest, we should have a chat. And if God is leading you elsewhere, at least you'll feel more certain of the path you're on." He started a conversation with a nun, keeping an open mind. He had made no commitments; he had only initiated the relationship. The more he explored, the more he was interested. And the more he was interested, the more he explored. Today he is "Father Matt," and has been a priest (and a crowd favorite) for nearly six years. He loves what he does and has found his passion, but that passion didn't start as a burning fire; it started with saying "yes" to a conversation.

His love for dance followed a similar path. He didn't wake up one morning and say, "I want to be a breakdancing priest" (though that would have been awesome)! It came from signing up for a talent show. Matt was watching a dance movie and thought it would be great to have a dance battle at the Seminary. When he started, he didn't even know how to do an 8-count, but he learned step by step. He now not only breakdances, but is proficient in hip hop, modern dance and ballet. But this huge passion started with a fun idea and the decision to follow it.

Matt is fluent in Spanish and has a huge heart for Latino Americans, but he didn't know that at the beginning of his seminary experience. It started when he got involved in a mission trip to Mexico. He figured, "If I'm going to Mexico, I should brush up on my Spanish." His fluency grew and his commitment to the people increased because he could hear their hearts more directly. Now over half of his homilies are in Spanish, but his passion started with a decision to dust off his language skills for a trip.

Another friend and role-model of mine, Steve, has accomplished a feat that very few people have ever dared to consider—he ran across the entire country. That's not a cute way of saying that he ran a race in every state. He actually ran across the U.S., from Los Angeles to New York City (à la Forrest Gump), in five months. Doing this required that he run thirty to thirty-five miles a day for five days a week, which means that on average, he ran *a marathon a day for one hundred days*. Steve runs with an organization called Team WorldVision, which provides clean water for villages and communities in Africa. He has personally raised (and has organized groups which have cumulatively raised) over $1.3 million for clean water in Africa. Obviously, this cause is something he is very passionate about. But he was never passionate about running!

He ran his first marathon at the urging of a friend to help raise money for WorldVision. He didn't feel like it, but he thought it would be for a good cause. After he had a decent experience with it, he committed to doing another. After that, he committed to bringing someone with him.

Over 150 marathons later, Steve Spear still does not feel like running, but he is passionate about changing lives, partnering with his organization, and doing what he feels God has called him to do. He found one of his life's passions after he committed to taking that first step.

1° Off: Passion Doesn't Come First

"I don't know if I'm really passionate about that" has become a trendy and cool-sounding way of saying "I just don't feel like doing that."

Too often, students mentally check out of class because they aren't passionate about the subject matter. But maybe if they got involved, paid attention and tried, they would find something that would spark an interest in them. At the very least, they might become smarter and more capable of accomplishing something later.

Too often, people pass on opportunities in life simply because their initial zest for the endeavor waned. But, if they had a good initial response to the opportunity, there was obviously a spark there. Don't over-think things; just get involved. In the words of Nike: "Just do it." Or, take the risk of becoming a slave to your emotions.

We shouldn't make decisions based on feelings alone, but rather should make decisions based on creating a positive difference for the future. If it's a good logical move, or even if it simply interests you, commit to starting and take it one step at a time. Get started, because the passion you're looking for may be just a few steps away.

Passion follows commitment—not the other way around.

Chapter Review

Delusion: I should feel fully passionate before I pursue something—because everything starts with passion.

Reality: True passion is the end result of going after something with everything you've got.

63

Delusion #4:
You Must Be Passionate About the Process

Mark Nathan

At twenty-one years old, I began to dislike looking in the mirror. All the late-night diner hangouts, the all-you-can-eat cafeteria buffets, and an erratic exercise schedule had caught up with me. I decided it was time to start losing some of my "college fifteen." I was determined to start eating better and go to the gym more often, but as many of us know, that's much easier said than done. Though I was initially inspired by my health-kick resolution, the process of forming habits to lose weight was riddled with mental struggles:

"This meal bar isn't very tasty, maybe I should look for one I'd like better."

"This treadmill is boring."

"Going to the gym is not very convenient for my schedule."

True, a protein bar is not as tasty as a Snickers bar, but my desire to have everything taste like a Snickers bar is the reason that I needed to lose weight.

True, all workouts are not exciting, but while I waited for a fun boxing class or workout DVD, I gained more weight than I wanted to lose in the first place.

True, working out did not conveniently fit into my schedule, but my need for convenience made me take the elevator instead of the stairs, which ironically necessitated the twenty minutes on a Stair Master.

I hadn't gained the weight (and then struggled to lose it) because life is enormously difficult. Rather, I finally learned that my thought process was what was causing my problems! I was focused too much on enjoyment and not focused enough on accomplishment. Life is tough, but it's tougher when you're focused on the wrong things.

1° Off: There's Always Boring Stuff

In the last chapter, we discussed the "1° Off" principle as it relates to the role of passion when starting new endeavors. We know that passion is an ingredient for success, but we're a little bit off on when to look for it. Most think there must be a deep feeling of passion *before* starting a new project or a new chapter in life. In reality, passion is not a prerequisite for beginning anything.

Feeling passionate is much too unstable of a foundation to make long-term decisions. The best time to evaluate your passion is *after* there has been involvement, commitment and accomplishment.

But what about *during* the process?

Let's rewind back to a time you were excited about something new. Maybe you watched the Olympics and wanted to learn a new sport, you saw a movie and wanted to be more of a tough guy, or even saw an infomercial with some new cleaning gadget and got inspired to clean your place. Often, we have an abundance of inspiration and excitement at the beginning of a new project—but what happens shortly thereafter? The answer: we get bored.

After the initial excitement wears off, what we're left with is boring stuff. The mundane work that is not nearly as fun or simple as the movie or infomercial made it seem!

This frustration with the process, a.k.a. the boring stuff, is where we're 1° off. We believe that when we've discovered our passion, there won't be any more mundane moments! We believe when we're truly passionate about something, we will love every second of what we do. Passion will turn that frown upside-down, and every menial task will somehow feel like the most meaningful moment of our lives. Long hours and sleepless nights will be filled with joy and happiness—heck, we won't even need coffee because we're so high on life!

It's a nice thought, but that's just not how it works. When encountering something new, many people never start because they're afraid, but just as many people get started with passion and then quickly quit when they arrive at the part of the process that takes work. They are focused on the process and convinced that if they were on their right path, it wouldn't feel so hard.

The focus needs to shift, or we'll never make it to the finish line.

Focus on the Finish Line

I recently saw a YouTube video of a company interviewing candidates who responded to a job posting titled Director of Operations. During the interview, the candidates were informed of the numerous and very intense job responsibilities: planning, organizing, maintaining, individual coaching, dealing with conflict, actively working eight to ten hours a day, few breaks, and being on call 24/7. At the end of the interview when the candidate asked about salary, they were told that there would be no pay. "Who would do that?" and "Are you crazy?" were some of the typical responses as all the candidates absolutely turned down the job. In actuality, it was a commercial lauding the billions of mothers who actually do that job everyday. Moms voluntarily do their "job" not because they're thrilled by the day-in, day-out routine of being a mom, but because of the end result of raising a wonderful child.

"Everything meaningful has stages of drudgery and stages of triumph. It has a beginning, a struggle and a victory." That statement was made by a man named Mahatma Gandhi. Personally, I would rank Gandhi pretty high up on the list of people who lived their lives with purpose and passion. With the weapons of peace, love, and sacrifice, he fought for an India free from British rule and in doing so, inspired the entire world as

67

well as generations to follow. But even one of the most passionate men in recent history knew that neither every moment nor every task would be sunshine and lollipops.

Gandhi's quote says "...stages of drudgery and stages of triumph." There's nothing that sounds fun about drudgery. It sounds like a lot of work—and boring work at that. It sounds slow, painful, and uncertain. But you don't start anything focused on drudgery and struggle; you focus on triumph and victory.

Very few people actually enjoy writing papers and studying for tests (I say a few because my wife is one such person), but they do enjoy the accomplishment of getting a good grade and being one step closer to their future. If that's what a student wants in the end, she'll pick up her book and study. When I was rehearsing for shows, I didn't like enduring long nights, memorizing lines and continuously running through scenes. However, I did like the idea of putting on a great show that would entertain a lot of people. I liked telling a story that was awesome and inspiring. So I got on the train and went to rehearsal. I ran the lines over and over and over again. I sat through seemingly endless nights of rehearsal to make sure that we would create a huge success on opening night!

This theme of focusing on the finish line is present in every industry.

My wife was in a writing workshop with Tony Kushner, one of the most renowned playwrights of his generation. Someone asked him, "Mr. Kushner, what do you like most about writing?" His answer surprised her. He said, "I don't like to write. I like *having written*."

Mr. Kushner didn't fall under the delusion that to accomplish something meaningful, he would have to be passionate about the act of sitting at a table and writing until his hand cramped. He wasn't trying to find soul-stirring inspiration in the process of staring at a screen until his eyes hurt. He wasn't so deluded to think that all of the workshops and endless drafts of stories were supposed to be magical and brilliant. Like all accomplished people, I'm confident he did those things for the end result: the satisfaction of writing something that he cared about.

Passion in Action (a.k.a. The Boring Stuff)

The truth about passion is that it drives you, but it doesn't eliminate the fact that accomplishment is a process, not an event. Passion is always found in the achievement, but is not always found in the work. Unfortunately, most people think that they have to be passionate about every second of the work to achieve anything significant. Those who don't find a way to accept the drudgery will always find themselves wanting something more. Real accomplishment will only belong to those who understand that real passion will be saved for the end.

Passion is always found in the achievement, but it's not always found in the work.

Bradley Cooper was asked about his incredible performance as real-life war hero, Chris Kyle, in *American Sniper*. Cooper said in an interview about finding his character, "You just keep doing the work. Every day, every day, every day...and all of a sudden, he was there. And that was a wonderful feeling." Notice: Cooper didn't say that the work every day, every day, every day was a wonderful feeling. He said the result of finding his character was a wonderful feeling.

The need to be able to visualize and focus on the finish line has been a constant theme in my own life. At nineteen years old I landed a role in an educational film about the diversity of Canada. Filming was in Vancouver, and it was my first time visiting the city. The days were long, but one night we were given the evening off, so I decided I'd watch the sunset. I walked along the English Bay downtown and absorbed the scenery.

Vancouver is a spectacular place: a beautiful coastal city on the Pacific that is framed by a mountainous backdrop. The city "pauses" in the middle, having dedicated hundreds of acres to a forest preserve. It is every bit a city and at the same time an earthy oasis from urban chaos.

I found a seat on a log (dozens of these lined the beach for use by pedestrians to take a rest and enjoy the scenery). As I watched the sunset, I looked out over the water and at the buildings surrounding the beach, and then saw something I'd never seen before. On the penthouse of one of the buildings a large circular balcony jutted out from the terrace. And growing out of that balcony was a live, fully-grown, sprawling oak tree.

I knew nothing about the building or the people who lived in the penthouse, but it struck me as so unique that it must be owned by some movie star or extremely wealthy and successful individual. A vision in my mind started to grow about the type of wealth and lifestyle I could have in my future: the cars I could drive, the vacations I could take and the homes I could own. It suddenly dawned on me that I didn't have to stop at one house! Sure, Chicago would always be my home base, but I was growing quite fond of Vancouver as well. And now that I'd thought of it, Barcelona, Tokyo and Australia also seemed to call to me. Maybe I could have five homes located strategically around the world?!

Now, let's not mince words. If all this sounds materialistic or like I was obsessed with money, it's because to a certain extent, I was. Growing up in my pre-teen years, my family had a certain amount of financial comfort and security. My mother and father, who had immigrated to America from the Philippines and Burma, respectively, had come to the U.S. to pursue careers in medicine, and together enjoyed a nurse/doctor income and lifestyle. However, all that changed at twelve years old when my father went into business with some shady doctors who were doing illegal billing. My father, though a brilliant physician, never felt he had a head for business and didn't looked into their practices, preferring to focus on his patients instead. When the other doctors in his practice got discovered and taken down, he got taken down with them. He lost his license, and all of a sudden our family went from a nurse/doctor income to just that of a nurse.

My mother and father were determined that their children's upbringing would not change because of this. They had come to America for a better future for their family and they made sure we still had all the opportunities they could muster. They refused to sell the house. They wouldn't take us out of private school (even though we never knew how we were going to pay for the next semester). My mom worked overtime and double shifts for the better part of a decade trying to make ends meet. Their diligence and determination was remarkable, and it paid off! They kept their home and provided an incredible education for their children! But the flip side of the coin was that my mother was absent and/or exhausted most of the time, the family finances were always strained, and we lived in a constant state of wondering how we were going to pay bills, the mortgage, tuition, etc.

I understood money wasn't the secret to happiness, but I'd already tasted what a lack of money was like, and was pretty confident that wasn't the secret either. I knew that I wanted prosperity to be part of the future I was pursuing, and at that point in my life I felt confident that acting was how I was going to get there.

Later that summer I was performing in an unpaid, non-Equity show to build my résumé in the theatre world. The fact that it was unpaid was not a small thing to me. Though my vision for prosperity was clear, I was still completely broke, and every dollar counted. On the side of that show, my film partner Jon and I had received a grant for a short film, and were in pre-production. We were auditioning roles the following day and I had in my bag all the résumés and headshots from our hopeful actors.

After rehearsal was over I went to a nearby diner with some friends and left my bag at the theatre, letting some key people know I'd be back for it soon. However, by the time I got back, the theatre was closed and locked (though I'd been assured it would still be open). I tried to contact someone to let me in, but no one was answering the phone. I knew I needed my bag for our auditions the next day, which meant I would need to go home and then come back the next morning.

The problem? To come back the following morning would require four transfers on the Chicago Transit Authority: a bus and an el ride, and then an el and a bus ride. But I only had enough left on my CTA card for one ride plus two transfers, which left me one leg of the trip short. I was so completely and utterly busted that I didn't have the extra two dollars to my name to purchase that final leg. So instead of hopping a bus to get me from the el stop to the theatre the next morning, I walked/ jogged the two mile stretch in ninety-nine degree heat. By the time I arrived at the theatre, I was furious: I'd wasted my time and was running late, I looked and smelled disgusting, and I wanted a Snickers bar like nobody's business. But I couldn't even afford that! My hungry brain started entertaining thoughts about how much money I could be making if I would have pursued a summer job instead of this theatre project. I wasn't used to being paid nothing for my time. Suddenly, the path from where I was standing to rich and famous movie star hanging out under a tree on a penthouse balcony in Vancouver seemed like a long and arduous road indeed.

And that is the moment that many people quit.

Thankfully, I never let my brain get to the stage of seriously considering jumping ship. Despite my complete frustration, I understood that enjoying the process wasn't necessary for me to succeed. If I was ever going to bring to focus that vision that was in my mind, certainly there would be long and thankless days while I was getting there. I kicked out my emotions and let my sense of duty to my dream run the show, and I decided that I didn't necessarily have to enjoy the process to be committed to it.

At the core of every passionate endeavor is a mundane process.

While building my businesses, I've had to relearn the exact same lesson. I was excited about income potential and opening new doors in my life, but I couldn't have been less enamored with the process. I was passionate about the idea of creating a cool event or prospering financially, but that meant doing the legwork of creating a functional business! In any business, money is made when purchases happen—tickets are bought or products are sold. The problem was, I had no sales experience and didn't like selling. I learned quickly that people won't purchase anything if they don't know what you have to offer. And certainly, no business will grow if you don't talk to people about what you're doing! That meant I had to identify the added value to customers and learn a sales pitch. I had to be disciplined to make calls and be accountable to weekly goals for myself. I was passionate about succeeding, but I had to accept and even get excited about the boring/scary parts of the process. After years of focusing on the "grunt-work", I created enough financial opportunity to call my own shots at twenty-seven years old. Now, I'm very passionate about spending my days however I want!

At the core of every passionate endeavor is a mundane process.

As any organization grows, one must learn how to scale so they're not limited to only their individual time and effort. I was passionate about the idea of leading a team, but that meant that I had to create one! Since no one in the world is exactly like me (thankfully), I had to learn to deal with different types of people. Everyone has different goals, personality types, strengths and communication styles; which meant I had to sharpen my people skills and read lots of books. This was tough for me; I'm very much an "action" person who would rather be out accomplishing something than sitting in one place reading words on a page. But I committed to the process of learning, and started tearing through books from relationship and leadership experts.

I learned that communication is not really about what you say, but rather about what the other person hears. I was a driver, an organizer and a delegator. I was used to being in charge and telling people what to do. I liked to be communicated with efficiently, and so I naturally communicated to others in bullet points. What I didn't realize was how many people I was turning off by doing this. To them I sounded bossy, pushy, or like I didn't care about them. It didn't matter that in my heart I cared a lot about the people I worked with; my style of showing it made my intent indecipherable. I had to learn to see things from the other person's perspective, and adjust my own tendencies to prioritize my effectiveness with people.

I was passionate about being a leader, but part of leading means learning to motivate, inspire and bring the best out in people. As an actor, I could basically operate as the center of my own world, and I was quite comfortable relying on myself to get the job done. But as a leader, I had to learn to inspire productivity and enthusiasm. And to do that, I needed to find other people's strengths and hot-buttons. I'll admit that initially, I had a hard time recognizing strengths in others if they weren't similar to my own.

For example, I am very good at seeing the big picture. But if someone else was very good at seeing tiny details, I didn't view this as a complementary strength and a great addition to the team. Instead I wondered why they were so dense that they couldn't catch the vision, or I'd get frustrated with their dedication to boring minutia. After having met hundreds of people and reading dozens of books, it finally dawned on me that my strengths weren't someone else's weaknesses. And even more of a revelation (since I never struggled with confidence) was realizing that other people had strengths where I was naturally weaker! Learning to identify what makes each individual special and finding how they can contribute to a larger team-atmosphere is now one of the most exciting things that I do!

Though learning people skills, communication styles and strength-finding could often be frustrating or feel like a waste of time, I was committed to the process. I didn't need to feel passionate about every moment along the way, because I was passionate about the outcome. And ironically, my dedication to this passionless process prepared me for the most passionate relationship of my life. My wife, Meredith, has a completely different personality, set of strengths and communication style than I do. While I am project-oriented, she is people-oriented. While I prefer bullet points, she can sit and talk to someone for hours at a time. While I am bold and loud, she is bold and quiet. And if I hadn't learned to deal with people who were different from me, I might have completely missed her. Today we're very blessed to lead *together* hundreds of people, helping to bring out their best and encourage accomplishment in their lives.

The Secret to Getting Through the Boring Stuff

I never liked the idea of having to do anything boring. And I was really talented at avoiding things that I didn't want to do. Often, I'd spend so much time thinking about how to avoid the work that if I actually just did what I was trying to do, it would have been done already.

Human nature is basically this: people do what they're good at, and avoid what they're bad at.

I abhorred writing papers in school, so I avoided them like the plague. I was a champ at taking tests, doing equations, and giving presentations, but I would always get lower grades on papers. I'd spend hours trying to think about how I could procrastinate doing the work, because I was simply not good at it. Along the way, I learned how to write in a way that worked for me (I'd talk through the ideas and adjust the thoughts into words on paper) and I started getting faster at it. I learned how to close papers in a way that was productive and got a better response. I got better at writing effectively and it became less of a chore.

I spent a lot of time avoiding making phone calls as I grew my businesses because I just didn't like making them. I would worry for ten minutes about what the person on the other end would say or how the conversation would go. But if I'd just have hit the call button, the conversation would have been over five minutes ago! The bottom line was that I didn't like making phone calls because I didn't know what would happen. So I learned to accept the fear and move forward anyway. I also learned how to ask questions that guided the phone call in the direction that I wanted it to go. I sent myself voicemails so I could hear what I sounded like on the phone, and would adjust over and over until I sounded like someone I'd want to talk to myself.

I didn't like making phone calls, but today I'm confident on the phone and am comfortable talking to anyone. I didn't like selling products, and yet today I've helped to build a number of successful businesses. I never liked writing, but here I am writing a book.

If there are parts of the process that are boring or frightening, and yet are necessary to accomplish the things you're passionate about, my recommendation is that you get good at them.

When you get good at the skills it takes to get through the boring stuff, you'll get through the mundane process faster and develop some very useful skills along the way!

The Passion, The Plan, and The Process

What's the end result you're after? You'll need a plan that can get you there.

How do you execute your plan? You'll need a process that works.

The hardest part of pursuing any passion is found in the acknowledgment that every moment may not be fun, but that doesn't mean it's not incredibly important.

Every step of the process may not move you in the deepest part of your soul, but each step is absolutely crucial to creating a life you're passionate about living. Remember, you don't have to be passionate about the process; simply be passionate about the results, and do the work to get you where you want to be.

As many have said before—the only place success comes before work is in the dictionary.

Chapter Review

Delusion: If I'm not enamored about every detail, it must not be my calling.

Reality: Be passionate about the rewards and results, and stick to the process that will get you there.

Delusion #5:
Living Passionately Is All About You

David Anderson

How much money would it take for you to be happy? One hundred thousand dollars? One million? One hundred million? One billion? What number would you choose? Why would you choose that number?

During my tenure at J.P. Morgan, I was an analyst on an individual's investment portfolio that was worth $110,000,000. I should also mention that it was a liquid portfolio of $110,000,000, meaning that the money could be accessed in cash within seven to ten days. This was all owned by one person—wow!

What are some of the things you could do with $110,000,000?

- Your family could live on two-percent investment returns that would yield income of $2,200,000 per year.
- You could run for president of the United States (paying for your own campaign).
- You could purchase a dozen McDonald's franchises.
- You could buy a few private jets.
- You could send 550 students to Harvard University tuition-free.
- You could feed 5,000,000 U.S. households for one year.

Obviously, no one has sympathy for a person who is unhappy when he has $110,000,000, but that doesn't stop a person from being unhappy. I've seen it! But why?

In 2010, there was a Princeton University study by Daniel Kahneman and

Angus Deaton which found that at the national level, making more than $75,000 per year (U.S. average income aggregated over fifty states) won't significantly improve your day-to-day happiness.

What?!!!

Yes, it's true. Your emotional well-being will not drastically improve with more money beyond certain income levels. As a matter of fact, many people experience more hardships as they make more money, especially if they get a lump-sum all at once. Think about all of the lottery winners, professional athletes and entertainers that receive mega-millions in a single contract. The world celebrates with them and they believe they're on top of the universe. Within a few years, we often read about them being broke, busted and disgusted. Most of the stories are pretty similar when people are asked how they lost so much money: "I didn't know I had to pay so much in taxes" or "All of my family and friends started asking for money all the time" or "I invested a ton of money in a bad business deal" or "My girlfriend/boyfriend took money from me without me knowing" or "My lawyer and financial advisor cleaned me out." My favorite is, "I thought money would make me happy, but it didn't; so I'm depressed!" I guess the poet Notorious B.I.G. was right when he wrote: "the more money we come across, the more problems we see."

So if money won't make you happy, where does happiness come from?

True Happiness Comes from Relationships

I'm reminded of a Fortune 500 executive I befriended about five years ago. He was the CEO of a major multi-billion dollar corporation for fifteen years. I heard him speak at an event and asked him out to lunch. He was the first Fortune 500 executive I had met up to that point that hadn't emotionally attached himself to money, his company's success or the Wall Street reports, even though he had every reason to do so.

When he joined the company, it employed only seventy-five people. By the time he became CEO, they employed 3,000 people, and when he retired it had grown to 30,000 people and generated billions in revenues worldwide. What he told me has always stuck with me: he said that after all of the success he had achieved, the day he left the company as CEO, it was all over. He didn't receive invitations to the hottest events in the city anymore. No one was seeking his advice on company growth or emerging markets. Even the Christmas and birthday cards diminished.

Fortunately, he had learned that the true secret to happiness wasn't found in the money. During his tenure as CEO, he made sure his success was benefitting his family. Also, he made sure that he and his wife had family dinners together at least three times a week. He scheduled all of his children's important events so he didn't miss them. He shared the company profits with all of his employees so that his success enriched the lives of those working around him. And this final one floored me when I heard it: he was part of a group of married friends who had met biweekly with their spouses for thirty years—and they were still meeting!

He had discovered a vital truth: no matter how much success, money or accolades you acquire, it's the relationships you build in life that bring you happiness.

Why Following Your Passion Brings Happiness

This isn't a message about making time for family, although I believe family is a vital component to happiness and should be a priority. Just as certain people believe money will bring them happiness, others believe the same thing about passion. Like getting to the right income bracket, many think that if they find the right job or calling, one they're passionate about, then happiness is sure to follow.

But following your passion doesn't bring you happiness just because you're doing something special for yourself, much the same as acquiring a certain amount of money won't bring fulfillment all by itself. The big mistake people make with passion is focusing too much on what's happening on the inside, instead of what's happening on the outside.

79

The big mistake people make with passion is focusing too much on what's happening on the inside instead of what's happening on the outside.

If you follow your passion for music, do you only play for yourself or is the goal to play for and delight others? Are you passionate about art in the hope that your work is put away in storage or do you want it in a gallery for people to see? Your passion is only truly fulfilled when what you're doing has an equal effect on someone else. When a song you wrote helps a young girl through a difficult time, that's what you're really passionate about! When a video you create reaches thousands of viewers and makes them laugh, that's what gets you excited! Feeling like you've added value to the lives of others is what makes you feel valuable. It's your gifts, talents and heart *in the service of others.*

Your Life Affects Others

I wrote previously about my decision to go to college, despite a stormy home life. At the time that I graduated from Chicago State University, I was the first person in my family to have completed a college education. Then I went on to be selected for a new program they were piloting at Harvard called the Diversity and Explorations program. It was a multi-faceted exploration of the intersection of religion, business ethics and politics. I was one of a fifteen-person cohort that got to interact with some of the smartest minds in the country, and was dedicated to solving problems and creating change in the world. The value of that program (our lecturers, visiting professors and the mastermind of students I was a part of) made an unforgettable mark on me. I drew inspiration, values and purpose from that group that are still with me today. What I didn't know was how my decision to go to school, and then to be a part of this program, would have a ripple effect on those around me.

Several years after completing Diversity and Explorations, my aunt Jasmine reached out to me regarding her daughter Tia. Tia was making her mother extremely proud. Tia was smart and motivated. A junior in high school, she was gifted in mathematics and was excelling academically. Despite some less than ideal family circumstances while growing up, Tia was at the top of her class (at this writing, she has the second highest GPA amongst her classmates).

Tia had been asked to write a paper for the National Honor Society about inspirational people and role models in her life, and her mother invited me to their home to read her finished project. I said I would and looked forward to it; after all, I've had many of my own role models who have inspired me along my path (Martin Luther King, Jr., Abraham Lincoln, Victor Franco, Billy Graham and Mother Theresa, to name a few), and I love watching the positive impact that a good example can have on someone's life path. As I sat in Jasmine's living room and started reading this document, my mouth dropped open and my face started to flush—the role model she was writing about was me.

I had inspired her to work hard and do well in school. *I* had inspired her to want to go to college. *I* had inspired her to believe she could really succeed in a future career. All of my accomplishments, all of my pride and sense of self-worth that I had built up over the years of fighting battles and facing personal mountains all seemed to fade into nothing terribly important. I was floored. The truth is that I've rarely had a more validating moment than when she told me through her written word that I'd added value to her life, my example had benefitted her, that I'd encouraged her and given her hope, and that I was part of the reason that she was choosing to pursue a successful path in life instead of the path of so many previous generations of her family.

Your passion is only fulfilled when what you're doing has an equal effect on someone else.

To this day, when I'm doing outreach work with my church and I have a chance to interact with young kids who share with me a similar upbringing, I frequently wear my Harvard t-shirts. At first, my wife Kristin was very uncomfortable when I'd do this. She thought I was bragging. But the truth is that I wore the shirt to let whose kids know that no matter where they came from and no matter who they were, they could make it to the school of their dreams. They could achieve high levels of success, and the good things in life weren't just for somebody else—the good things in life were for them.

Life Is More Awesome When It's Not About You

I don't write any of this to toot my own horn. I'm actually writing from the perspective of being a very selfish person. At our most instinctual level, I think we are all self-focused until we make the conscious choice to be focused on those around us. But I had a longer road to travel than many. Having been raised in chaos (I've already mentioned the poverty, the divorced home, the schizophrenic mom), I grew up with a focus on survival. I couldn't count on a benevolent parent to look out for my best interests, so I decided early on that I needed to watch out for me and mine.

I became involved in a gang, not because it was best for the community around me, but because I was looking for a feeling of belonging. I started to do drugs, not so I could be a more productive member of society, but because drugs made me feel good (or at least they gave me a break from the pain of daily life). Eventually, I started to sell narcotics and put together a larger business plan to make these deals even bigger; I didn't do this to enrich the lives of my customers; I did it because it was lucrative. My heart was hard. I was angry at everyone. I was at an all-time low. That was the person I had become, that was the person running my life in the summer of 2001, and that was the person who answered the phone one morning when my grandmother called me.

"David, where are you at?" I answered vaguely. She persisted. "You need to go to the hospital to visit your mother. She might not make it."

My mother was in the ICU at the time, battling leukemia. I dutifully went to see her, and was relieved to find her sleeping. I looked down at her, hooked up to a breathing machine, and quite possibly on her death bed. But instead of feeling love or sorrow, my heart was filled with hate, confusion and frustration. And I remember only one thought going through my head: if she died today, I really wouldn't care.

Several days later, I was on the porch drinking and smoking weed with a friend of mine, Mary. All these thoughts started running through my head: about life and death, about heaven and hell, about God. I started asking her questions: was God real? Was hell real? Was the devil real? I guess she wasn't in the mood for introspection.

"You're just tweaking, David...you've had too much to drink...calm down."

I told her that she didn't understand; that life sucks! I wasn't getting any answers from her, so finally I told her I was tired, excused myself, and walked off the porch. I pointed my finger up to the sky, and said out loud, "God, I'm about to go down a path that's not gonna be good. Man, I tell you what: God if you're real, if you...are...real, I need you to show yourself to me."

The next day I was at school and a classmate invited me to a pizza party. I knew he was religious and the party was going to be religious, so I made up an excuse not to go. After school he tracked me down again, and again I resisted. Finally, he got me to come. At the party, over a slice of greasy pizza, he looked me dead in the eye, and said with a peace and conviction far beyond his years, "David, today is the day that you have to give your heart to God. Today is the day that He is calling you. You have to give your heart to God."

I was floored. My heart welled up with awe and wonder. When I looked into my classmate's eyes I could see the eyes of God staring back at me. I knew this was more than just a coincidence or a religious student on his soapbox yet again; I had called out to God in angry desperation, and He had answered back. I knew with complete certainty at that moment what I had to do.

Two weeks later, on September 11th, two planes crashed into the Twin Towers, and America would never be the same. But I was already not the same, and instead of doing what I would have been doing (dealing drugs or getting high), I was leading our entire school and the surrounding region in prayer for the families and victims of 9/11.

My whole life I'd wanted recognition, fame, and respect. But I'd wanted it for my own gratification. Now I was on CNN and in the New York Times, as this prayer movement was broadcast around the country, and I couldn't have cared less. I was on fire for the Lord. I was fulfilling His calling. I was trying to listen to His voice and be obedient to His calling as to what I could do to help strengthen our grieving nation. It was the great awakening of my life. I was a boy who was filled with hate and anger, who didn't care if he hurt his community, who didn't even care if his mother lived or died, and who thought he knew all he needed to know to be happy. But I transformed into a young man who understood that he was part of a bigger picture, who found his happiness in finding ways to add value to those around him, and who found his purpose in giving himself to God. And I've tried to let His voice guide every decision I've made ever since.

Two weeks after that fateful pizza party, I was leading my whole region in a prayer movement that got broadcast across the nation. One week after that, my best friend Chuck smoked a joint laced with chemicals, and just like that, he lost his mind, never to retrieve it.

That would have been me sitting there next to him, smoking that joint...*if I had still been living a life focused on me.*

1° Off : *Your Passion Is Not About You*

We started this chapter talking about money. On either end of the money spectrum, money won't bring happiness. Being rich doesn't automatically bring happiness, and being broke doesn't necessarily bring unhappiness. We understand money is important, but we're a little off on how and why it can create happiness in our lives. In a similar way we know passion and happiness are tied together, but are 1° off on the connection.

Money is a tool. What do you do with a tool? You use it as a means to an end, not an end in itself. With tools, you can accomplish things that you have no way of doing on your own. That's why you see great people who make lots of money creating foundations and contributing to programs that change lives. Money is a tool to help you positively affect other people.

Your passion is a tool. Your unique passion is a resource that helps fuel your ability to add value to your world. If you pursue your passions hoping it will bring you happiness, you will never be happy, because living a life of passion is not about you.

Relationships are what bring happiness. Affecting people in positive ways brings happiness. If you try find your happiness by being selfish or hurting other people, any enjoyment you derive will be temporary, and ultimately very lonely.

Money and passion are both important, but you don't see their ultimate value until they are focused properly on other people.

It's not about your talents—it's about your talents in the service of others.

It's not about your gifts—it's about your gifts benefitting others.

It's not about your accomplishments—it's about how you can help more people with your new mantle of success.

Money and passion are both important, but you see their real value when they are focused properly: on other people. Don't become emotionally attached to money or passion, because when you chase either, you'll be chasing them the rest of your life. Chase purpose and live a life that's bigger than you; when you do that, *passion will find you.*

Chapter Review

Delusion: Following my talents and strengths at all costs will make me happy.

Reality: Your talents and strengths, in the service of others, will make you happy.

Part I Review:
The Delusions of Passion

David Anderson & Mark Nathan

At this point, we've assured you that living a life of passion is very real and awesome, but we've also pointed out some ways of thinking in our own lives that we realized were taking us down the wrong path.

We've introduced the "1° Off" principle: the further you plan to go, the more damaging 1° off in your plan becomes. If you have small things to accomplish, being a little off course may not cost you much in the long term, but if you want to accomplish HUGE dreams, being 1° off could change everything. Being 1° off could mean the difference between creating a dream life—or living a nightmare.

We've identified that pain is not a bad thing. If life seems more difficult than you expected or you're pursuing something that not everyone understands, it might be painful dealing with that hurt or rejection, but that's normal. Growing pains are part of the process of pursuing your passions, not a sign you're on the wrong path.

We've acknowledged that problems come with the territory when you move forward in life. In fact, dealing with your current problems is how you move on. Your current problems are not cramping your style; they're opportunities to grow and develop yourself into a more capable individual to succeed at an even greater level.

We've realized that feeling passionate is not a prerequisite to starting something new. Actually, feelings in general are a very unreliable way to make decisions, especially potentially long-term decisions. If a new project makes sense for your future, get involved and see if doing that evolves into commitment and accomplishing bigger things. Passion is not the beginning, but rather the end result of giving something everything you've got.

We've understood that the process will have its boring periods. There can be no expectation that every minute of your work will translate into constant rainbows and ice cream. Working a plan and executing the process will not be thrilling, but that's what passion (in action) looks like. Don't focus your attention on the process; focus it on enjoying the end result.

We've recognized that going after our passions will not make us happy. Developing our passions so we can positively impact other people is what will make us happy. Relationships and being interconnected produces real fulfillment—not being in a life-long, self-focused pursuit to find personal happiness. Passion, like money, is a tool to benefit other people and the world around you.

Why Start With the Tough Stuff?

We're not a fan of lectures and we've done our best to make sure this book doesn't come across as preachy. That's not where our heart is. We are so excited to see millions in our generation rise up and live amazing lives and we know that means more people operating at full capacity ASAP. So now we're ready to focus on Part II: the action steps to creating a life of passion.

Let's use a simple example. Would you trade someone else's one hundred dollar bill for your five dollar bill? That's a no-brainer for sure. But if they tried to hand you a one-hundred dollar bill, and your fist was clenched shut grasping on to a five-dollar bill, you wouldn't be able to take what was being given to you. You would be so consumed with hanging on to what you have that you couldn't grab hold of anything new!

Your mind works the same way. Growth, change and open-mindedness are not always the natural state-of-minds. Rather, train yourself to loosen up on the mental death-grip on how you think—so you can receive something new.

88

That's why we took the first half of the book to debunk some commonly-held delusions that people have about passion.

You can't grab on to new stuff until you let go of the old stuff!

We all want so badly to make the most of our lives that we have very deep-seated feelings about living our dreams and passions. If we don't loosen up on our ideas about chasing our passion, or on the clenched fist we have on our current plan, we may miss out on some pretty amazing stuff!

So before we move on, let's be very clear about one last item that we've already talked about a few times, but bears repeating. It is the foundation of everything.

Let go of this: *You will one day find your true passion and life can really begin.*

Grab on to this: *You will create a life that you are passionate about living, with every decision you make, every day.*

There are two key words in that sentence to explore before we move on to Part II:

You Will **Create**...

This means that your life is uniquely yours. The life you live should not be a cookie-cutter life that leaves you constantly comparing yourself to others or wondering if you're missing something. Even if your life has seemed pretty standard up to this point, after this book you'll be in create-your-life mode and you'll realize you're in a real-time, choose-your-own-adventure book.

When you're in create-your-life mode, you'll be the person that everyone loves checking in on to see what you've been up to. Your profile will be the one people want to explore on social media. It's a journey you'll look back on and love because, truly, no one else could have lived that life except you.

You

No one else can create this life of awesomeness except you. Until now, you may have spent your whole life letting other people call your shots. In high school, you just have to show up and try to feel like you're progressing. College gives you a little more independence, but ultimately still provides a structure within which to operate. Some people even start their working lives just doing things because it seems like the smart or normal thing to do. But it's not your parents', teachers', friends' or boss' job to make your life count.

You are responsible for maximizing the talents you've been given.

You are responsible for exploring the things that interest you.

You are responsible for the relationships in your life.

You are responsible for the life you live every day.

That may seem like a lot of responsibility, but it's thrilling! If you are responsible, that means you don't have to wait on anyone else to start creating your perfect, unique and amazing life!

You *will* ***create*** *a life that you are passionate about living, with every decision you make, every day.*

So let's equip you with a few thoughts, ideas and tangible next steps as you create a life this world has never seen...

This life is uniquely yours.
You are creating a life the world
has never seen!

Part II:
Creating a Life of Passion

Create Your Life:
Resolve and Refuse

David Anderson

Jack Ma, founder of Alibaba, the largest online retailer in the world, has one of the most fascinating stories of the twenty-first century. He grew up poor and malnourished in China. His only possibility of economic mobilization was to go to college, but he failed the college entrance exams twice and his parents discouraged him from taking them a third time. Afterward, he tried to get a job but no one would hire him. In order to learn English, he would give free tours to English-speaking tourists in exchange for English lessons. He started two internet ventures before Alibaba that failed horribly. Unlike most of the successful business men in China, Jack Ma had no government connections or wealthy elites to support him and his dreams. All he had was a dream of building something in China that had never been built before. At the time, China had a huge challenge with both consumer and business-to-business trust using e-commerce, so Jack Ma created a way to guarantee payment for and delivery of products, and his company was a huge success! Emerging out of a communist country, Jack Ma was the antithesis of a typical Chinese success story in the early 2000's. So much so, that even I thought his story might have been fabricated for purposes of propaganda. But it's all true.

Today, Jack Ma's company Alibaba is valued at $231 billion, with 20,000 employees and over 100 million users on its site; twice the size of Amazon and eBay *combined*. How did Jack Ma accomplish so much? How did he keep his resolve during all of the rejection and failure? I believe Jack knew what he wanted and what he didn't want.

Passion can get you excited about a decision, but it doesn't help you stick with it.

One of the challenges in operating from passion alone is that it's an entirely emotional experience, and success isn't emotional. In fact, achieving success is mostly mental. Passion will usually get you excited about a decision, but it doesn't help you stick with it. The thing that helps you thrive beyond passion is knowing what you want and what you don't want.

Jack Ma had a deep resolve to achieve the things he wanted and an even deeper commitment to refuse the things he didn't want.

Resolve: What Jack Ma Wanted

- To speak English
- To learn to operate in the Internet world
- To create a company that allowed small businesses in China to trade goods and services online
- To create jobs and opportunity for people who didn't have any
- To prove that anyone could succeed in a communist country like China

Refuse: What Jack Ma Didn't Want

- To live in poverty
- To be illiterate
- To be a failure in business
- For China to be known as a country where only the privileged and elite could succeed
- To let down all of the people who believed that he could create something great
- To fail in trying to make a difference for his generation

Resolve

One of the most intriguing aspects of someone when they have resolve is that they can almost seem a little too sure of themselves, a little too motivated, a little too illogical (and even unreasonable). That's because resolve only occurs when you have really thought deeply about the "why" behind your actions. You've contemplated the purpose, dissected the obstacles and calculated the risks. Resolve isn't a fleeting feeling like a firecracker which makes a large BOOM, sparkles and then fizzles away. Rather, resolve is like the stars of the galaxy which burn day and night, no matter what.

When you have resolve, you are relentless in your pursuit and purposeful in your journey.

Resolve will wake you up early in the morning and have you stay up late at night. Resolve will make you love unconditionally and hate justly. Resolve will push you, move you, lift you, build you and inspire you to greatness. Resolve helps you reach your greatest potential in your life.

But here's the tricky thing about resolve: you have to have seen something, in your life or in your mind, before you can know if you really want it. Napoleon Hill said, "What the mind can conceive and believe, it can achieve." If success is mostly mental, you have to have the picture of where you're going clearly etched in your mind.

Resolve in Action

I remember when President Obama was elected to the White House. It was a huge inspiration to me, as well as to many other African-Americans and Americans in general. The moment he was inaugurated, I knew I wanted to work for him. I even said it out loud: "I'm going to work for President Obama one day." The only problem was that I didn't know how that was going to be possible.

Soon after that I met a young man with a lot of authority and power named Robert. Robert was my boss at Goldman Sachs, and was one of the most fascinating individuals I'd ever met. Half-black and half-Jewish, Robert grew up in California and moved to New York for college and grad school.

By the time he was twenty-one years old, Robert had completed his B.S. and his M.B.A. from Columbia University. He then became the youngest consultant to enter McKinsey Consulting, a global management consulting firm that serves businesses, government and not-for-profits. He participated in multiple programs to serve under-privileged and under-served communities.

After working with McKinsey Consulting he went into investment banking, became a White House Fellow during the Bush administration, and then the Chief of Staff at Goldman Sachs, all by the time he was thirty years old. As if that wasn't enough, Robert had also run fifty marathons in fifty states, started a charter school, and started a not-for-profit that helps first-generation-American college students get corporate internships to get exposure (an organization that serves 200 students yearly, and for which I now sit on the board of the Chicago branch). When I met Robert, he was twenty-nine years old, and I'd be lying if I didn't admit that my first reaction was to be intimidated. I practically wanted to re-enroll myself in kindergarten. It was like he had accomplished in ten years what might take someone else ten lifetimes. But meeting him was one of those defining moments in my life, because *it let me know what was possible...*

Meeting Robert furthered my inspiration and my focus to work at the White House. Though he was my boss, I pressed him with questions to find out how he'd managed to accomplish something that might as well have been going to the moon in my mind. Hearing his stories and his climb to success made a big impact on me: as I've already mentioned, what the mind can conceive and believe, it can achieve. It's not a mystical saying; it's a law of success. My mind became like an antenna sorting through signals in my daily life, zeroing-in on opportunities. I was fixated on my new resolve: to get to Washington.

I started meeting people that had worked at the White House, and everyone I met, I interrogated for knowledge and clues. I learned that of all the 400 employees that work at the White House at any given time, a whopping thirty-three percent are interns. I realized that from a numerical perspective, the intern approach was my best bet for getting there (even though I already had a well-paying job). I also learned that you have a two-year window after graduating from college to apply, but once you've submitted, it's a rolling application. I learned about the types of people they like to bring in—and about the types of people that they don't. I learned what values were important to them: community service, a life that's committed to the public and a good work-ethic with a healthy dose of ambition (but not TOO much ambition; they like their interns grounded, safe, and unlikely to end up in the news!).

I applied, reapplied, and applied yet again. After a period of time, I finally got called in for an interview. After four or five interviews, a contingent offer, and an eighty-page background check, I was brought in as a White House intern.

I was put in the front office of administration and instantly had quite a bit of responsibility. I worked hard at my position and played my part. I made friends with my colleagues and did my best to add value and make a good impression. Nothing was too small a task for me; I was simply grateful to be there! My vision and resolve had finally come to pass: I was working for the president, just like I said I would. Soon afterward, I was promoted from a White House intern to a White House Associate/Aide. When I met the president for the first time, I knew that I had earned my right to shake his hand by being resolute.

Refuse

While resolve has to do with a deep commitment to attain the things you want, refusal is the grounding mechanism of knowing what you don't want. While resolve will motivate you, refusal will mature you. Refusal is harder to understand because it requires a certain level of experience (and frequently the negative kind).

When someone has come out of a deep poverty, they are more likely to do whatever it takes never to experience poverty again.

When someone has been taken advantage of or cheated, they never want to be taken advantage of or cheated again, nor should they desire to make someone else endure a similar ordeal.

When someone is diagnosed with a terminal disease because of being overweight, they will cut out junk food from their diet, exercise every day, and spend thousands to regain their health—if they refuse to endure those same health issues again.

While resolve is usually born out of passion, refusal is typically born out of pain. That's why you cannot resist pain, heartache and difficulty. Like we talked about in earlier chapters, it is vital to the process of success! It is the only true way you can build resolution so you know what you don't want out of life, which is just as important as knowing what you do want.

Resolve is typically born out of passion; refusal is typically born out of pain.

Refusal in Action

Just as my resolve got me into the White House, there were certain things that I was determined to refuse in my life when I came out. Though I'd met many incredible people there who were smart, hard-working, charismatic and wise, I also saw a common theme among certain interns that demonstrated to me the person I didn't want to be.

I saw patterns of entitlement, especially among those who had used family connections to gain their position.

I saw twenty-four year-old interns that had researched and prepared information for certain policies, who then became indignant because they weren't invited into the meeting to discuss the policy with the president. I saw young men and women upset because they weren't instantly granted high-level positions in their first corporate jobs after leaving the White House, and resentfully accepting middle-management jobs. In one situation, a CEO of a Fortune 500 company was in town, and asked to be given a tour. I was asked to be the tour guide, and I eagerly accepted. After all, I hoped that I could glean some small nuggets of business wisdom from this man as I spent several hours with him. I prepared and arrived early so I could promptly start the tour—when one of the staff members told me to hold back.

"Why did you need me to hold back? Is there something you need me to do for you? This CEO is waiting for his tour..."

"Let him wait. We work at the White House. He doesn't."

Perhaps it was how hard I had worked to get to where I was. Perhaps it was because I had no family connections to get my foot in the door. Perhaps it was because I was still unaccustomed to being in the presence of great men and women, but seeing some of my colleagues acting with so much arrogance and self-importance gave me the resolution to always keep my appreciation.

I *refused* to lose my humility.

I *refused* to think I was better than anyone else.

I *refused* to act like I had arrived, but instead resolved to stay on the journey.

I decided to treat a crumb like a feast, even while watching others do the opposite. Even on days when I didn't feel passionate about the job I was doing, when it felt too menial or mundane, my refusal to think myself too important for a job kept me on the right path, being the person I'd resolved to be.

Back to Jack

Jack Ma is known as a really fun and unconventional CEO. He celebrates his employees' marriages with a grand wedding ceremony at the company's offices. He holds concerts at corporate headquarters for staff and encourages people to have time with their family and not just work.

He seems to be the picture of a highly successful individual living a highly passionate life. During a *60 Minutes* interview he was asked why he treats his employees so well. He said, "Ten years ago when the country was hit by SARS (Bird Flu), all the employees in the company were quarantined and I was locked in a room for ten days, but when I left the room I said to myself, 'Life is so short, so beautiful. Don't be so serious about work. Enjoy your life.'"

We can derive a lot of meaning from that statement and endlessly discuss what Jack Ma really meant, but it was only through his resolve (knowing what he wanted) and his refusal (knowing what he didn't want), through his vision for his future and through his failure and pain, that he was able to create the life he was truly passionate about living.

You and I have the same choice everyday: to live life only by passion, or to live with resolve and refusal.

Because life is so short, and so beautiful.

Chapter Review

Create Your Life: Resolve & Refuse

Action Items

Over the next five years, what are five things you would like to accomplish?
(e.g., work for the president, start a business, write a book, etc.)

_____

_____

_____

_____

_____

Lisit three people who have experience in these areas, from whom you can seek advice.
(e.g., boss, former teacher/professor, friend, etc.)

_____

_____

_____

What are three personal traits/life situations that you refuse to allow in your life?
(e.g., paycheck-to-paycheck living, no relationship with parents, still living in the same neighborhood, etc.)

_____

_____

_____

Create Your Life:
Develop Daily Habits

Mark Nathan

I loved college. There was so much to learn, and it seemed that in every moment my mind was being stimulated by some exciting activity, enriching association, or scintillating debate. I was exposed to so much knowledge: from reading Plato's *The Allegory of the Cave* and exploring the Socratic Method of Learning in the morning, to learning about the rivalry between Shakespeare and Marlowe in theatre history in the afternoon, to swapping stories at night with a friend from my class on the Golden Age of Rome and his class on the Beatles, my mind was on constant overload in the best possible way.

Those four years also allowed me to have a lot of very formative experiences and great opportunities. As a young educator, I began as a school tutor but ended up creating an after-school drama program, helping to start an arts summer camp in the city, and working with one of the best children's theatre groups in the state. As a young actor, I had paid my living expenses during school doing acting gigs, I had founded a film festival, and my developing professional career had upward momentum. There was a lot to be proud of, especially since I had just started performing after high school. On the outside, everything was moving forward quite nicely.

But on the inside, I felt very differently. Over those same four years, I had become a different person than the one I'd been in high school. I'd made many choices that I was not proud of, especially the morning after. Most weekends, I spent my nights in some sort of stupor, which earned me a reputation as someone that others could only conditionally trust. My moral compass was pointed in whatever direction that suited me at the moment. I was very talented at rationalizing my behavior and convincing myself and others that I was still a good person overall.

I was the guy persuading others to be irresponsible with their studies so that they could come out and have fun. I was the guy that encouraged you to let your morals slip a little bit. I mentioned earlier that during college, I realized I'd stopped looking at myself in the mirror...my freshman fifteen was only part of the reason why. The person I was becoming was going down a very different path than I would have anticipated four years earlier.

Shortly after graduation, I was sitting at a conference learning about my new business venture when I heard a statement that changed the entire course of my adult life: Hell on Earth is the person you are meeting the person you could have been.

I related all too well. I understood immediately how fast a person's potential and their reality could be moving down totally different paths. As a young professional, I was very proud of what I'd accomplished; but as a young man, I was very ashamed.

Hell on Earth is the person you are meeting the person you could have been.

Deciding to Change

No one likes to change—because change is not an easy thing. By definition, you have to leave something that you're used to, something you're comfortable with, and traverse into something unknown. That's why most people won't change under normal circumstances, even if it's a smart idea.

But change in your life is inevitable. In fact, the only thing that never changes is that things are always changing! "Adapt or die," as Billy Beane (portrayed by Brad Pitt) says in the movie *Moneyball*. So if life is constantly changing, and we need to adapt (but no one wants to change), how do we get ourselves moving to keep up with life?

Ideas don't move people, emotions do. People don't begin losing weight because it's the logical thing to do. People change their exercise and dietary habits when they're sick of their clothes "shrinking," or they become unhappy with what they see in the mirror. Selfish people don't change how they deal with people because the golden rule just makes sense; they learn to treat people well when they get tired of feeling lonely and watching movies late at night by themselves. And most people won't decide to better themselves, further their education, or pursue new opportunities out of a dedication to self-enrichment; rather, they do these things because they feel stuck, trapped, and can't get ahead in their career.

When it hurts badly enough, you'll decide to change.

That quote about the definition of hell did that for me. It hurt to think about it. It reminded me of the man I wanted to be when I was younger:

I wanted to be someone who could be counted on in times of need.

I wanted to be someone who could be trusted with anyone/anything.

I wanted to be someone who not only was going to win, but whom others wanted to see win.

During college, I went from those wonderful ideals to becoming someone my family wouldn't be proud of and becoming a man that I never intended to be—and I suddenly realized that I wanted to change that. Maybe that sounds very idealistic. But maybe the world we live in has gotten all too good at rationalizing broken values, just like I had.

The Reality of Change

Deciding to change is hard. Being patient enough to change is harder.

Because I didn't lose my way in one day, I wasn't going to find it again that quickly. Change is not an overnight accomplishment. Change is planned. Change is patient. But ultimately, change is simple.

Famous author, speaker and pastor, Jerry Seville, once said, "If you want to change your life, just change something you do consistently, every day."

If you eat brownies every day, you'll very likely gain weight. If you change from eating a brownie to doing a set of pushups every day, you'll get stronger. If you look at women the wrong way every day, you'll turn into a jerk. If you stop ogling girls by reminding yourself that this girl is someone's daughter or wife, you'll start to develop a respect for people you were previously objectifying. If every day after work you turn on the television and watch it all night long, it's very easy to become mentally passive, lazy and dull. But if you stop turning on the television and instead open a good book or call up a friend to have a conversation, you'll stimulate your brain and start learning new skills that will make you sharper.

Do you see the crucial component? The pattern in successful change lies not in elimination, but in replacement. Bad habits are tough to eliminate, but easy to replace. Good habits are hard to establish, but simple to substitute.

Deciding to change is hard. Being patient enough to change is harder.

Replace Your Furniture

Imagine that you are looking around your home one day and decide that you're sick of your old furniture. Your chairs have springs poking through holes in the fabric. You table is covered with water stains, and it wobbles when you lean on it. Your bed smells funny, and it isn't all that much more comfortable than the floor. In a fit of disgust and inspiration, you decide to get rid of all of it, and you throw all your furniture into the alley. Congratulations! Your negative circumstances hurt badly enough that you decided to change, and you took immediate action to get rid of these problems in your life. And for the first few moments after this passionate fit, you feel very good about yourself. So what's the problem?

You are now standing in an empty house. You have successfully discarded all the old stuff you didn't want. But what happens as that feeling of conviction for change starts to fade, as you stand in the middle of your empty living room?

How long will it be before your feet hurt and you start thinking about one of your chairs outside? What's the likelihood that before the end of the day, you'll bring a chair back in from the alley so that you can sit down? And what happens when it's time to eat and you miss your table? Maybe for the first meal or two, you'll enjoy the novelty of your picnic-style dining, but within a few days, don't you think you'll bring that wobbly table back in? Then at night, when it's time to sleep, what happens when your mattress starts to sing to you from the outside? It wasn't much more comfortable than the floor, but now that you're actually on the floor, you realize it wasn't that bad...and slowly but surely, you bring back all the stuff you were very determined to get rid of in the first place!

Let's rewind, and go back to before you went crazy and threw out all your furniture. What if when you realized that you wanted to get rid of your chair, you ordered a new one? What's the likelihood that you'd go and bring back the old chair from the alley? If you replaced your table the second you tossed the old one, or had a new and better mattress before nightfall, would you even be thinking about your old stuff?

The hidden secret to creating a better life is changing your daily habits.

The hidden secret to changing your daily habits is replacing habits you already have with better ones.

The changes I made were small initially, but meaningful. I replaced my Saturday night shenanigans with sports activities, game nights, and movie dates with friends. I began seeking out great new relationships with people who weren't engaged in a lifelong competition of idiocy. I replaced some useless and/or negative online habits with books that had subject matter about which I was actually excited to learn.

I realized that when I was proactive about replacing old habits, making better choices was not really that hard! These new habits were really starting to take hold, and I got excited.

Develop Habits That Get You To Where You Want To Go

Let's tie this into creating a life of passion, in case you haven't already connected the dots.

The U.S. Dream Academy, a nonprofit organization that works with children of incarcerated parents, focuses on helping those kids develop a strong dream for their future. Founder Wintley Phipps has stated, "When you've got a dream that you are passionate about, you're going to develop the character it takes...you're going to search for the skills that you need [to accomplish it]. You become like what you see unless you dream."

When you know what you want, and when that want is important enough to you, you'll change into the person you need to be in order to accomplish your goals.

To create a life you're passionate about...you will need to develop into a better version of yourself.

Creating a life of passion looks different for everyone, but one commonality is that you will need to develop into a better version of yourself than you currently are. That's why we talked about change. That's why we talked about habits. In creating a life you're passionate about, you will need to grow and develop yourself daily.

Some of you already have a profession, line of work, business or craft that you're excited about. If you don't have that yet, think about the things you're good at. What things bring you joy or make you feel the most fulfilled when you do them? Are there specific things you feel called to do? Are there skills that you can develop that will help you become better at those things? Are there some personality quirks you should work out or people skills that could help you excel? Or perhaps, like me, some of you have changes that need to be made having to do with character.

Identify areas of personal and career growth that will help you succeed at the next level. Then break down those areas of growth into daily habits. Next, figure out how to incorporate those habits into your daily life. What you do every day is what shapes your future.

Big changes stem from small habits.

Tips to (Successfully) Create New Habits

There's no doubt that developing productive and sustainable habits is the biggest determining factor in how you become the person you would like to be. At twenty-one, I wanted to draw a line in the sand and become that person as fast as possible. Let me give you a couple of tips on developing habits that will actually produce the change you are hoping for:

Tip: Start Small

Big changes stem from small habits. Leadership expert John Maxwell often talks about how committing to five simple actions every day created the foundation for everything he has accomplished (which is extensive). I think five simple habits is a phenomenal place to start, and something that everyone can do. How do you choose what habits to start with? Most people pick habits to help them fix some of their biggest problems. But here's the challenge with that: your problem areas are problematic to you because you have trouble with them. I'm not suggesting you avoid dealing with your weaknesses, of course, but if you spend all your time focused on things you're bad at and don't like to do, you won't have a shot at doing them consistently.

If you are trying to develop five habits, you should pick a few that address weaknesses you need to shore up, but also pick some that develop your strengths. Developing strengths is a good way for you to gain momentum

109

with your habits (versus the natural tendency to procrastinate working on your problem areas).

By coupling the weaknesses you must fix with the strengths you can't wait to develop, you put yourself in the best spot to create effective change.

Tip: Attach It to Something Else

My wife has an incredibly disciplined habit of listening to audios every day. Whether they are leadership teachings, sermons or personal-growth audios, every morning there is something blasting throughout the Nathan home. It wasn't always like that, though.

Meredith would listen to audios in the car, but since her schedule wasn't fixed, it wasn't happening as consistently as she wanted. If it didn't happen during a car ride, she would try and fit it in later in the day, but it was pretty hit-or-miss. But then she simply attached her listening habit to something else she was doing consistently everyday: showering! So, every morning when she started getting ready for the day, she'd listen to her audio. Simple!

Can you attach the habits you're trying to develop to something you already do every day? If you can (whether you attach it before, during or after the habit you already have), you'll find that sticking to new habits is pretty simple!

Tip: Don't Overwhelm Yourself

Many people have a hard time sticking with new habits because they make the same rookie mistake I did: they try to take on too much at one time. I thought I could fast-track becoming a better Mark by working on more areas of my life and developing even more change.

I wanted to become more financially disciplined, so I set goals for myself in that arena. But then I realized that I wasn't working out as much as I wanted to—which meant that I had to make better choices in terms of my physical fitness. Meanwhile, I committed myself to being a better son and returning my mom's calls, going to church every Sunday, and reading the bible every morning.

I was throwing out more furniture than I was able to effectively replace. My very small, simple changes quickly escalated into a full-scale financial, physical, spiritual and relational renaissance. Well, everyone knows what happened next. My inspiration lasted for about four days. I followed up with some of my new habits the next week, but by week three, it's like none of it ever happened. Which makes it difficult to change because...

Tip: Consistency is Everything

As many times as I've played soccer in my life, you'd think that I'd at least be a decent or competent player. But that would be a very bad assumption to make. All of the games I have ever played have been small pick-up games at summer barbeques or late night with some buddies, and while I've played many times, there has never been a period of time in which I played consistently. That's why I never got better.

You can't master anything you do occasionally. Nowadays, I play football as infrequently as soccer, but remain pretty good at football simply because I played consistently for seven years growing up.

After ten days of trying to develop your new habits, take a very honest evaluation of your consistency. If you are not impressed with your performance, something needs to change.

The most crucial part of developing yourself isn't picking the perfect habits, it's doing them daily. If you haven't been able to stay consistent with five simple habits, maybe you need to start by adjusting the plan to do two habits consistently. Again, if you are going to pick two things to work on, pick one that addresses a problem area, and pick one that develops a strength. It's better to start with two or three habits you do consistently—than five you do occasionally.

You can't master something you do occasionally.

Tip: Tell Someone

In 2011, I gave up desserts for an entire year. It wasn't necessarily a health or a diet thing; for me, it was about discipline. I've never met a dessert I didn't love, and when I was looking to develop overall discipline in my life, I looked for a couple of areas where I could get some wins under my belt. The second I decided that I was giving up desserts, I knew I needed to tell people.

The more people you tell about your habits, the more accountable you become. Most are afraid to tell others about their goals because they're afraid of failing. What I found is that the more people you tell about your goals, the more likely you are to accomplish them. The day I made the decision to give up desserts, I told people *that night.* Many of my friends had the same look on their face—a combination of disbelief and a smug look of certainty that I would break within a week. Their judging me (politely) was part of my motivation to help me get over the initial hump of the new discipline. Over the first month, as I saw more of these people, they would ask how the "dessert thing" was going. It became a built-in accountability reminder to have a number of people aware of my intentions.

Tip: Talk about It Often

Many people don't want to talk about something before it's a reality. They want to shock the world and surprise everyone with their accomplishments. As I built my direct-sales business, my initial goal was to give something back to my mom for all the years of hard work and sacrifice she gave to our family. I knew that when the money started coming in, I would bless her with gifts. But I talked myself into not mentioning it to her, because I wanted to surprise her. What I was really doing was giving myself an out in case it didn't happen. The more you talk about anything, the more convinced you become. If you are waiting for other people to encourage you, you are missing out on a huge piece to this puzzle. The person you hear more than anyone else is you.

If you are encouraging yourself and talking about your goals and habits often, you become your own best motivator. What would happen if you mentioned to one person everyday about how you read every night? It would only be a matter of time before you consistently read every night. Even if you missed a night, but mentioned the next morning in conversation how you read every night, it wouldn't be very long before you got yourself back into that habit. The more you talk about your daily habits, the more likely you are to really lock them in. The more you talk about a goal, the more conviction you have for accomplishing it.

The more you talk about a goal, the more conviction you have for accomplishing it.

Replace Your Furniture Now

Too many people lose time getting ready to get ready. Though we can't rely on inspiration and passion to get started, they are great accelerators when you have them, and can help you fly past procrastination, excuses and the thousands of distractions that life will throw at you between today and tomorrow. A friend and mentor of mine, Dr. Robb Thompson, often says that the most crucial time that determines someone's progress is the time between knowing and doing. It doesn't have to be perfect, but it does have to start.

The person you are can become the person you want to be. Developing consistent habits is what will help you forge that path.

Chapter Review

Create Your Life: Develop Daily Habits

Action Items

What are two bad habits you'd like to replace? What new habits will replace them?

(e.g., late-night eating, inappropriate websites/movies, swearing too much, lying, etc.)

_____

_____

_____

What are two skills that you can develop that will help you accomplish your goals?

(e.g., better phone skills, efficient planning, organizing events, etc.)

_____

_____

_____

What daily habits can help you develop those important skills?

(e.g., reading aloud, planning your day, networking daily, etc.)

_____

_____

_____

Create Your Life:
Surround Yourself with Amazing People
Mark Nathan

As much as I don't want to admit it, I'm not really as awesome as I believe I am. I have a pretty healthy self-image and frequent fantasies of grandeur. I've spent my whole life believing I was meant to do something great and that I was destined for leadership. I have always been sure that my wife would have unending love for me, my kids would look up to me as their hero, and my impact on the world would be so large that the ripple-effect would reach my great grandchildren. But what I've come to realize is that every goal I've set, every proud moment I've achieved as well as everything I plan to accomplish in the future all have one thing in common: I'm not good enough to do any of them on my own.

The thing about "The Story of Your Life" is that it's less about you than the title might suggest. True, it's your time and your choices, but the fact of the matter is that we live in a world where we are dependent on each other. No matter how awesome you are, you can't get through life as an island. And the bigger your goals and dreams are, the more reliant on other people you'll need to be.

Always Tied to Other People

Leadership expert Dr. Robb Thompson says it like this: "At the end of the day, we are not independent people. We are interdependent people." You only have to pay attention to the details in our everyday life to see how true that really is.

From the moment I wake up in the morning and go into the bathroom, I'm dependent on the great people at the water company to make sure water comes out of my sink when I turn it on. I have the same dependence on the electricity company, the phone company, and the wonderful people at Netflix who enable my binge movie-watching habits. I don't see any of these people face-to-face, but my daily living depends on them doing their jobs miles away from me.

I'm also dependent on people with whom I have direct contact as I go about my day: the barista at Starbucks, the cab driver and the office manager at work who does something important (though I can't say what, exactly). These people can affect my attitude, change my perspective and influence how much (or how little) I accomplish during my day.

We can't function in life for very long without dozens of daily interactions with other people, but obviously some of those relationships are more impactful in our lives than others.

None of us are independent people; we are all interdependent.

The Big Relationships

The maintenance worker in your building could do something to affect your water pressure one morning or the barista at Starbucks could get your order wrong, but neither of these things is likely to change your world. Smaller relationships may have some impact on your daily attitude, but they have little-to-no impact on the overall direction of your life.

Even more defined relationships, though important, are not necessarily crucial to your success. An extended family member or even a brother could have an influence on you, but might not change your overall trajectory. Your co-worker that you sit next to or the person you've posted the most about on social media might rub off on you a bit, but that doesn't mean they are vital to fulfilling your life's mission.

However, a best friend that you see every other day or the person you run to for advice in your relationships—these people can have a huge influence on you. It's been said that you become the average of the five people you associate with the most. Dr. Thompson has also said, "You will share the deepest struggles but also the greatest successes of those closest to you." If you're very close to someone who doesn't want/expect more from life, you're tied to someone who may not have many successes to share.

When we talk about big relationships, it's important to clarify what we're talking about. These are the people with whom you are building your life. These are the people that will leave a lasting mark on you. These are the people who will change your life's course.

Everyone has big relationships in their life, but not everyone is intentional about developing them. And since big relationships have the ability to totally shift the person you are and the future you are walking into, doesn't it make sense to seek out and build the right ones?

Big relationships are crucial to develop—because success in life requires a team dynamic. Two types of big relationships that are vital to develop are partners and mentors.

Partners: Help You Accomplish More

Jimmy can mow a big lawn in three hours and Johnny can mow the same lawn in four hours—how long would it take if they worked together?

Do you remember these types of math problems in school? I always loved these equations because they revealed a basic truth that everyone inherently understands: we can accomplish more together than we can apart. Or, stated another way, we can accomplish more in less time if we work with a partner.

No matter what industry you are working in or project you are focused on, having someone with similar goals and commitments makes everything more productive, more efficient and more awesome.

When I would do short film projects in college, I had an amazing partner in my friend Jon. We were a great team. He was a film major at Northwestern, and handled everything behind the camera (lighting, cinematography, editing, sound). I handled everything in front of the camera (acting, design, production). Because of this complementary partnership, the short films we put together on a limited budget, limited time frame, limited technology and at a very young age are still impressive even a decade later.

The entertainment world is filled with amazing partnerships—people who attached themselves to each other and accelerated one another's careers: Martin Scorsese/Robert De Niro, Christopher Nolan/Christian Bale, Tina Fey/Amy Poehler, Jimmy Fallon/Justin Timberlake, Judd Apatow/Seth Rogan, Tim Burton/Johnny Depp, Matt Damon/Ben Affleck, and the list goes on. Their creative talents complemented and fueled one another. They often came out of nowhere and rose to the top very quickly, largely due to their dynamic partnerships.

Successful businesses often start with two people who have complementing strengths.

Successful business often start with two people who have complementing strengths. Apple is the biggest U.S. company ever, but began in a garage with Steve Jobs and Steve Wozniak. Rich Devos and Jay Van Andel accelerated the direct-sales giant Amway into what it is now, in over one hundred countries and territories. Ben Cohen and Jerry Greenfield gave us Ben & Jerry's Ice Cream (and subsequently contributed to my "freshman fifteen" weight gain in college).

As I transitioned from the arts into business, my friend Greg initially showed me the ropes. We both had a focus on accomplishment and a desire for world domination, but we had very different styles and personality types. His boldness and work ethic was a phenomenal balance to my vision and creativity. We added value to each other in tremendous ways for a number of years. Greg accomplished some very big business goals and I learned what it took to be a wingman, both of us accomplishing life goals along the way.

Our friends and business partners Derek and Jill were a great complement to my wife and me; they had different strengths and personalities, and added a phenomenal dynamic to our projects. They brought focus, drive and determination to the equation. We provided structure, guidance, and mentorship. We have accomplished many exciting things over the years, and Derek and Jill have created their own success, and an example that other people could follow.

In a similar way, we often see two dynamic business entities join forces to try to accelerate growth. In recent history, Lego has successfully partnered with major franchises to create age-appropriate video games (Lego Batman, Lego Harry Potter, Lego Star Wars, etc.) which then point kids back to the franchise-specific Lego block sets. Successful partnerships complement one another, create win-win situations and can multiply your results.

To be clear, I'm not suggesting that you have partnerships only because of the value they add to your life. Actually, I believe the opposite. I think your primary focus should be on the value you add to other people's lives (as we'll explore more in the next chapter). One-way relationships are a drain. Relationships that are functional and productive have to be a two-way street. In each example of partnership from my own life, there was time, love, servitude, mutual respect and sacrifice before relational reward.

Mentors: Help You Become More

Imagine you wanted to build a four-story mansion, but to save yourself time and money, you tried to build that home on the foundation of an outhouse. How effective would that be? A building is really only as good as its foundation, so if the foundation isn't strong enough to hold the house together, you'll have something that may look great but will inevitably crumble. That's exactly why your own growth is so important—your personal development is your foundation that will allow you to build up to even bigger accomplishments!!

Mentorship is the fastest way to accelerate your personal development.

Mentorship is the fastest way to accelerate your personal development. Someone more experienced than you who is interested in your success could definitely be a big relationship and has the potential to change the game for you. Someone who can give you practical and specific feedback on your day-to-day or month-to-month actions and help you see your blind spots is invaluable.

When I declared myself a theatre major at Loyola, my acting résumé consisted of one community-theatre show and a few high school video projects. Within a year and a half, I got an opportunity to audition for a minor role at a small, professional, non-Equity theatre. How did that happen at nineteen years old with less than two years of experience under my belt? I received invaluable advice from people I respected who had anywhere from three to thirty more years of experience and wisdom than I had. In retrospect, I realize that I essentially put together a board of directors for my career. You'll often see young athletes do the same. They have a trusted coach who brings out the best in them and guides them through their developing career. Eighteen-time Olympic gold medalist and world-record holder Michael Phelps has had the same coach, Bob Bowman, since he was only eleven years old, and refers to that partnership as "the smartest thing I've ever done."

In addition to learning valuable career and industry-specific advice from coaches over the years, I've also had mentorship that dealt with character and personal growth, and these are the nuggets that totally changed my life. For as many shining strengths as I possessed, I had just as many (if not more) glaring weaknesses.

120

Maturity

I was twenty and received a call from the San Francisco Shakespeare Festival to be their Genie in a holiday production of *Aladdin*. I was jacked. I was in my final year at Loyola University Chicago, and I had been performing in shows at school and in the Chicago area basically non-stop for three years. This was the biggest show I'd been cast in, and I was starting to feel like stardom was just around the corner. The theatre company flew me out to California to be part of the show, I was working with veteran actors who had been on Broadway and in national tours, and most importantly to me at the time…I was getting paid!

One thing I had learned in the theatre world is always to be working toward the next gig. Auditioning, networking and auditioning more…you always had to be thinking a few months ahead. So before I left for San Francisco, I let my theatre history professor, Professor Jack, know that I would love to be considered for a role in his next show. Auditions were happening while I was away, but since he knew my work from class and previous shows, he agreed to consider me without an audition.

During the next few months, my ego started getting a little inflated. I was reading my own press clippings (literally) and assumed that with all of my success, there would undoubtedly be a lead role awaiting my arrival in Professor Jack's next show. I received calls from classmates who wanted to know how I'd ended up on Professor Jack's call back list while I was on the other side of the country. That only fueled my confidence, and I went to sleep the night before the casting was announced beginning to recite lines in my head for the leading male role.

The next morning I received word that the casting had been posted. I called a friend and asked him to go to the theatre building and read the list to me. Starting at the top, he dutifully read each character's name and the actor who had been cast in the role. Down the sheet he went, line after line. And with every part and corresponding actor he read, my heart sank a bit. When was he going to read my name? Something was wrong. Wasn't I on the list?

Finally he got to the end of the sheet: ensemble. And there I was. I had been cast, but not in a leading role. I was baffled, confused and a bit indignant. Though you hear in the theatre world that there are no small parts (only small actors), I was sure this was too small a part for me. Confident that I could find something better, I turned down the role.

A few days after I returned, I got a call from the department chair, Sarah, inviting me to come to her office to see her. Sarah had already guided me through much over the years. She understood my ambition early on, helped me learn how to prepare for and balance…everything. When I wanted to start an after-school drama program, she pointed me to great resources and gave me tips on working with different age groups. When I wanted to start auditioning professionally, she gave me encouragement and feedback that helped me to bridge that gap. And to think I was one of many, many students in the program…Sarah's investment in me was truly amazing during my time at Loyola.

But when Sarah heard of my actions regarding Professor Jack's show, she was not pleased. She asked me into her office and immediately called me out for being a jerk. Of course, she didn't say it like that—her words were filtered through her grace, love, and tact—but the message was clear. When I asked for advice, she told me to own up to my actions—to make up for them, and to make the time count.

Sarah gave me a much needed wake-up call: I needed to be more responsible with my decisions, and also was reminded that I wasn't living on Planet Mark. What I hadn't seen through the fog of my career ambition was how classy Professor Jack was to have even considered me (absent that I was) for his show. I had disregarded how much thought and effort goes into every casting decision, even the "minor" roles. I was so consumed with my own ego that I wasn't thinking about anyone else but me.

I apologized to Professor Jack and asked if I could work crew for his show (since I'd already given up my spot on stage). Instead of being in the spotlight, I spent the run of the show in the sound booth learning to run a sound board.

I also took Sarah's advice to make the time count. Since I so arrogantly removed myself from Professor Jack's show, I felt I owed it to him to make sure those months were well spent. Two weeks after I made my apologies, we founded the film festival I mentioned earlier and went to work getting it off the ground. By the time the show finished its run, we were only forty-five days from the festival launch. Had Sarah not called me out, I might never have launched the film festival and my ego would have continued unchecked. Though it was a tough (and embarrassing) lesson to learn, I am so grateful for the perspective I received from a great mentor.

Servanthood

As you can probably tell, I had a slight tendency to come across as a diva. But in many cases that tendency was born out of my internal wiring for productivity (in addition to needing to get off of Planet Mark).

I remember being part of a director's forum my senior year at Loyola, where five student directors would meet twice a month to give feedback and learn from each other's experiences. On one of the days we were meeting, I was going straight from the forum to an audition immediately afterward. I realized just before our meeting that I had run out of headshot/résumés. The tricky thing about headshot/résumés at the time was that headshots were 8x10 and résumé paper was 8½x11—which meant that when you attached your résumé to your headshot, there would be extra paper to trim.

To me the solution was clear: I was going to this forum with five people, so if I could find a few extra pair of scissors, we could create an assembly line and crank out fifty trimmed headshots in less than ten minutes—the perfect plan!

Needless to say, my professor and other the directors were not amused with my assembly-line-during-class idea. The problem was that I saw people for how they could add value to my plans instead of trying to add value to theirs. That mindset won't take you very far in life…especially when you then get started in a business that requires you to prioritize other people's goals.

123

The online retail business I'd begun expanded by training other entrepreneurs, not by hiring employees. When hiring employees, it's much easier to make people listen to you, because you have the authority to sign their paycheck—and to fire them. But when you work with people on a voluntary basis and without such leverage, it requires you to connect with them in a way that is all about them—and not about you.

At a conference, I heard a man named Larry speak about being "others-centered," and what that looked like from a practical perspective. I never would have guessed that *he* would be an amazing example of servitude and selflessness. From my perspective, Larry was the big guy—the top man on the totem pole with a huge income and a fancy life. In my head, people like that had egos and authority complexes. I expected him to want people waiting on him hand-and-foot and bowing to his power and influence. So you can imagine my surprise when I saw him late-night at a diner, staying up a few extra hours to spend time with people who wanted to learn.

Since then, I've spent years learning Larry's personal history and watching him serve everyone around him. I found out that he didn't see his title and accomplishments as more reason for people to bend over backwards for him, but rather he saw his platform as a way to help everyone in his life at an even greater level, with a greater capacity. Larry truly embodied and demonstrated how to lead with a servant's heart. He helped change my inner-wiring from someone who saw people's value in what they could do for me to someone who actively looked for ways to add value to those around me. We should be excited to move up in life because that might mean that we will have a better opportunity to serve at a higher level.

When you move forward in life, it means you can serve at a higher level.

Opportunity beyond Ability

Often, a mentor can see talents and skills well before they have fully developed in a protégé. We can sometimes grow so accustomed to our own strengths that we underestimate what we can contribute to our environment. But with the much larger perspective that mentors provide, they can enable much larger opportunities in our lives.

After my co-author, David, finished his time in college, one of his mentors, Ernest, gave him an opportunity that some might have considered well beyond what he deserved for his years (this is the same Ernest of whom David spoke earlier). Ernest returned home to Chicago, after receiving his law degree from Harvard, to build a practice in his local community. Ernest met David through mutual friends and immediately recognized the desire for greatness in David's eyes. Even though he brought very little experience to the table, Ernest gave David the opportunity to help him build the operations and business side of his practice, and together they built the small law firm to over $1 million in revenue.

A few years later, Ernest decided to run for state representative. Again, knowing David's commitment to excellence, strong work ethic, and political savvy, he gave David the opportunity to help run his campaign. Unlike most in their mid-to-late twenties, he was not helping out or assisting…he was the campaign manager! Every facet of the election process went through him. Even though they lost the election, the experience is something that David has been able to learn from in order to accelerate his own journey through life.

Through a mentor's time and willingness to see you excel in life, you can stretch your abilities and develop stronger shoulders to carry more weight. But no matter how much a mentor sees in you or how many doors he can open, there is no replacing your own hard work. In fact, sometimes the opportunity to be mentored comes disguised as an opportunity to serve your mentor! Continue to earn your mentor's trust with hard work, perseverance and spirit of appreciation.

Different Seasons

As a quick note, some of your big relationships will change throughout your life. This should happen with much less frequency than some of your friendships in school or work, but just like all relationships, partners and mentors can come and go.

Some people are in your life for a season, some are in your life for a reason and some are with you from now until the end. Some partnerships can last your whole life, while others will help you grow and prepare you for your next chapter (and future partnerships).

Mentors are the same way. Some will be life-long and some will be there to provide wisdom and insight that will prove to be invaluable to you in the coming years.

Developing Amazing Relationships

So how do you develop amazing relationships? If you're like me, I figured out the power of surrounding myself with great partners and great mentors, but still had no clue how to find them. Where do these people live?

Live your life, be excited, and focus on what you can GIVE to the relationships around you. You will attract people who will then add right back to you. When you can be trusted with little, you can next be trusted with much, and a promotion to even higher levels of mentorship or partnership may be right around the corner.

You have strengths and a vision for your life that are unique to you. But I'd venture to guess that there are people going in a similar direction, with unique strengths of their own. When you combine your talents and abilities with theirs, you create a force bigger than either of you could have accomplished alone. If you have people like that in your life, continue to find ways to build and encourage each other. If you don't have people like that, find them. Again, the best way to find people who add back to you is to find people whom you can add to first.

You will share the deepest struggles but also the greatest successes of those closest to you.

You will share the deepest struggles but also the greatest successes of those closest to you. Being close to great people accomplishing great things is not an overnight process. It's developed over years of giving and adding to each other's dreams and goals. Start the process today, and start laying the foundation of your story with amazing people.

127

Chapter Review

Create Your Life:
Surround Yourself With Amazing People

Action Items

Who are two partners in your life who help you accomplish more?
(i.e. you're better together that you are on your own)

_____

_____

_____

Who are two mentors in your life who challenge you to become more?
(i.e. you have a relationship with them, they want you in their life & you want them in your life)

_____

_____

_____

How can you add value into the lives of these big relationships?
(i.e. what can you do for them that is unique & helpful to their calling)

Partner _____

Partner _____

Mentor _____

Mentor _____

Create Your Life:
Add Value to People

Mark Nathan

In the great state of Illinois, there are two major crops grown in the vast farmlands outside Chicago: corn and soy beans. As I started to develop friendships with people beyond city borders, I began learning about how incredibly detailed the farming business can be. From seed-coating to soil chemistry, planting depth to planting time—there are a lot of complex elements involved in growing a successful crop. You don't have to know much about the details of farming (certainly I don't), but there are two simple facts about farming that I think we can all understand:

1. If you plant corn, you will get corn.
2. If you plant corn, you will not get tomatoes.

There are certain ways the world works that will never change. No matter how much technology evolves, what happens in the stock market, or what is going on in your personal life—the truth remains that what goes in the ground is what's coming up.

This is also significant because based on that simple fact, we can reverse-engineer to gain additional insight. If you're buying a Christmas tree from a tree farm and you find yourself amongst rows of evergreens, you know what happened in that field years ago.

The field you're standing in reveals the seeds that were planted there.

129

You didn't see it, but someone put those evergreen seeds in the ground! Someone watered them. Someone tended to them. You know it without a doubt! If you're standing in a pumpkin patch, were carrots planted there the previous season? No! If you're standing in a field of pumpkins, you know that pumpkins were planted long before you arrived.

The seed you put in the ground determines the crop that will eventually come up, and the crop that eventually comes up reveals the seed that was planted there long ago.

Beyond Farming

We all know this principle reaches far beyond farming. Eastern religions refer to it as karma—everything you do will eventually come back to you. Judeo-Christian belief knows it as sowing and reaping—whatever you sow, so shall you reap. Scientists have Newton's third law of thermodynamics—for every action there is an equal and opposite reaction. This truth is hard-wired into the way the world operates, but do we allow it to influence the way we spend our time, the things we do, and our reactions to our circumstances? Farmers know to plant what they want to harvest, but do we understand and apply this same principle in our own lives?

I mentioned in an earlier chapter my family's tight financial situation as I grew up: a dual-income household reduced to one salary thanks to some misplaced trust and unfortunate relationships. We lived paycheck to paycheck, Friday to Friday. There was never really enough for...anything. And when there aren't enough resources, opportunities are limited.

I remember after my freshman year, my football coach suggested I work on my speed. I was decently quick, had big shoulders, and hit hard—which made me a solid fullback. For those that don't know football, a fullback's two main responsibilities are to block and to run people over. My coach believed that with more training and speed, I could be a force by the time I played on the varsity team. He suggested a speed camp that had produced good results for former players. I was very excited about being a better football player, but there was no money to send me there.

It was easy to blame our circumstances and put the fault on others, and if I'm being honest that's exactly what I did with my limited teenage perspective. But let's apply the farming principle to my family's financial situation. We were standing in a financial field of want. The field you're standing in reveals the seed that was planted and cared for, but also the seeds that weren't. So if we were standing in a field of financial... not much, guess what had been planted in the ground? Not much. My mom was working, but my father was tied up in legal battles and wasn't producing income. Of the money we did have, we didn't put money into real estate or other investments. We didn't try to create additional streams of income by building something for ourselves. There was no seed going into the ground, so how could we ever harvest a crop?

The best way to change the field you're standing in is to plant better seeds!

I learned this lesson growing up and was very proactive about having multiple streams of income early in my career. In my adult years I've learned to be mindful about making sure the seed I'm putting in the ground today is a field I want to be standing in tomorrow.

The Most Important Application

There are a number of ways that the sowing and reaping principle can manifest itself. The financial example is unfortunately all too real for many families. There are far too many fights in households about lack of money and not enough conversations about how to put better seeds in the ground! Another example is in athletics: successful athletes work hard in practice so when they dig deep for energy late in the game, they can reap the benefit of their extra efforts. Athletes that are lazy or short-cut their practice time will reap the *negative* results of their lack of effort.

But perhaps the most important area in which we should consider this principle is in how we treat other people.

No matter what profession you choose, where you live, or what you accomplish with your life you will have to deal with people. If you're an accountant and your best friend is a calculator, the end goal of those numbers you're working on is to provide information for people. If you're an artist up in a loft, ultimately you work to produce something that pleases and enlightens others. As we discussed in our last chapter, we are not independent beings, but rather interdependent ones—thus you will be interacting with other people throughout your entire life.

If interacting with people is to be an integral part of your life, you should get good at it as soon as possible. If I had known I'd be playing football off and on for the next twenty years when I started during recess in grade school, I probably would have worked harder on throwing legitimate spiral passes that first year, instead of throwing wounded ducks until high school. Knowing that I was going to be married to my wife for the rest of my life, I realized I should probably get good at understanding what makes her happy, sad and angry. I'll never be perfect, but if I could improve on some of these things in the first couple years of marriage, it would make the next few decades a whole lot more satisfying!

You will be dealing with people for the rest of your life. Every day. So why not get really good at understanding how to make dealing with people much more enjoyable and productive? Thankfully, the sowing-and-reaping/karma thing applies to working with people as well.

How you treat other people is a seed in the ground that will eventually sprout.

Never forget that how you treat people is a seed. To return to our farming metaphor, we all want to be standing in a field of amazing people. We all want people who care about us, people who are committed to us, and people who want the best for us. If you want to be standing in that field, you can do something about it today.

In the last chapter, we discussed what types of relationships to seek out to move your life forward. In this chapter, we'll explore how to create and nurture those relationships.

You can have amazing, positive, and productive people in your life...but it's all about how you treat the people in your life right now. Here are two principles to remember when it comes to working with people:

1. Avoid planting bad seeds
2. Actively plant good seeds

These two action steps may seem over-simplified, but they are incredibly powerful when remembered and applied!

Avoid Planting Bad Seeds

In the film, *The Departed*, we meet a young cop who is infiltrating the mob, and a young mobster who is infiltrating the police force. These were long-term undercover projects, so each man started out paying his dues in his respective field. Each had to move up in his fake life to accomplish his mission, and had to lie continuously in order to be promoted. The deeper into the lies each got, the more nervous they became. The more bad seeds they planted, the more they kept looking over their shoulders. Eventually, they both got what they knew was coming to them.

We should all know deep down that if we cheat someone, it will come back to us. When we deceive someone, we start a ticking time-bomb. So, we should try to avoid doing these bad things. This is a very simple concept and a well understood rule in all areas of society. In school, don't cheat. At work, don't cut corners. In relationships, don't betray people. Don't plant bad seeds, because they will grow to full harvest...probably at the most inconvenient time in your life.

But "bad" seeds don't have to be as dramatic as betraying someone's trust. If everything is a seed, then your attitude toward people is important to watch, too. What's your general demeanor toward people? Do you regard new relationships with skepticism and distrust? Do you see others as merely a means to accomplish what you want? How do you treat people who can do nothing for you?

I watched a family member go through an unfortunate harvest from some seeds he'd planted in his earlier years. When he met someone new, he would immediately measure them based on their education and profession. If he deemed them "lesser," his attitude toward them became one of apathy or disdain. He constantly treated people who were "below" him as though they were ignorant, and only considered them valuable if they were actively helping him with something. After many years, this relative hit a rough spot in his career. During those tough times, you'd think there would have been a handful of calls coming in (or calls he could have made) to try to help resolve the issue. After all, he was highly successful and well known in his field. But, unfortunately, no one reached out. No one bent over backwards to help him, because for years, he never really bent over backwards for anyone else.

This relative never actively destroyed anyone or did anything that would be considered wrong or bad, but his attitude toward people left a lot to be desired. He never saw people for how he could add value to them. Rather, he saw that people were in his way. Then, when he needed help, there wasn't anyone there for him.

Avoiding planting bad seeds is a huge key to success in creating good relationships. But you don't have to be planting bad seeds for life to get harder...life gets harder on its own. If you don't plant anything good in the ground, what comes up in an empty field? Weeds.

You don't have to actively plant bad seeds for life to get harder... life gets harder on its own.

Actively Plant Good Seeds

Everyone knows it's not nice to make fun of someone, but there is a huge difference between not being mean to someone and going out of your way to be nice to them. Of course, you don't take advantage of someone in a vulnerable spot, but is that the same as protecting them in their weaker moments? Sure, you don't betray a friend, but do you actively add to their dreams?

How fast would life move forward for you if there were people constantly looking out for you? Encouraging you and your ambitions? Doing everything within their power to help you win? Life would be great if people were adding value to you all the time.

If you want that harvest, plant that seed! Don't think about the return. Become obsessed with adding value to others!

If you want a great harvest from your relationships, become obsessed with adding value to others.

Three Steps to Add Value to People

<u>Start Small</u>

Look around. Every day someone is trying to accomplish something. Who in your life is important to you or is really going after something? What can you do to help them in their pursuit? Start with a handful of people who are right in front of you: your close friends, your boss or your spouse. Start looking for ways to support or encourage them.

I remember my friends coming to my first show after I decided to ditch the conventional Asian pre-med route in favor of acting. My family wasn't very supportive of my choice initially, so having my friends show up for me meant the world! Coming to my show only cost them one night, but I remember their gesture years later.

When I decided to get a film festival going in ninety days, there were plenty of people who said it couldn't be done in such a short time. But I clearly remember the handful that said, "If anyone can do it, you can!" When I launched my online retail business, the handful of friends that asked to be my customers were a huge support for me. Even if they only bought one or two small products, that little bit was a big confidence boost, and helped encourage what would eventually become a million-dollar-plus business enterprise!

135

If you aren't sure what you can do for someone, just ask! I'm sure it will mean a lot to them that you're looking for ways to support them—even if you aren't exactly sure how.

Ignore the Haters

The more you're involved in people's lives, the more you'll see how differently people respond to your actions. Undoubtedly, you will have people who will question why you're "being so nice." They will think you have an agenda or that you're trying to get something from them. Ninety-nine percent of the time, the reason they think that is because *they* have never done something for anyone else without an agenda. They cannot fathom the idea of simply planting good seeds for the sake of reaping a good harvest, with no ulterior motives.

What you'll find is that the most successful people tend to be the most giving. They make it a focus and a priority to find ways to give back to families, communities and organizations with their money, time or talent. Of course there are exceptions, but more often than not, they've adhered to these principles well before they started to "make it." They didn't develop a giving spirit after they had a lot to give; they developed their wealth *by* having a giving spirit.

Keep giving and adding value. Do it without an agenda—and you won't find yourself among haters for very long.

Help solve the problems of others— it's one of the most effective ways to solve your own.

Help Solve Problems

As Dr. Thompson says, "People will remember you most for the problems you create in their life—or the problems you help solve."

Everyone has problems they're trying to work through. From personal weight-loss goals to career advancement—those closest to you have things they're trying to accomplish right now.

Maybe a friend is trying to work at a specific company? Perhaps you can introduce him to someone who can help make that connection. *Don't wait to be asked—be proactive in developing these relationships.*

Maybe a relative just launched a new business? Perhaps you can support their efforts by actively finding ways to be a spokesperson for their goals.

Maybe your spouse is trying to learn something new? Perhaps you can take a chore off her plate so she has a few more minutes in the day. When my wife was helping to develop a skin-coaching program, she was running on empty nearly all the time. I'm no saint, but I just tried to help where I could *before* she needed to ask. I put a few date-nights on the calendar to give her a break and something to look forward to during the days that all seemed to run together. Doing these things gave her a bit of extra time, and also increased her clarity and focus while she was juggling a lot.

Helping to solve others' problems is one of the most effective ways to add value to their lives.

Avoiding the Pitfalls of Helping People

As you are finding solutions in other people's worlds, here are a couple of thoughts to save you from some potential dangers:

Help, Don't Enable

Solving problems does not add value if you're enabling someone's bad habits. There is a huge difference between financially supporting someone raising money for clean water in Africa versus financially supporting someone who blows their money on drugs/alcohol. They both have financial problems to solve, but the difference is clear. If helping someone enables their self-destructive behavior or hurts others, it's probably best to keep your distance.

Help Where You're Wanted

Don't invite yourself into your cousin's marriage problems because you can feel that he is struggling. If your friend has a baby, don't dub yourself her parental sage unless she specifically asks (if you do, you're not helping…you're being obnoxious). If you come as a guest into someone's home and start cleaning or reorganizing his things, you may have the best and most helpful of intentions. But the reality of the situation is that if you haven't been asked for help, you are simply being rude.

Help How You're Needed

Help in a way that is productive for the person you are trying to help. Perhaps she's raising money for a cause, but you're very tight financially. If money is what she needs most, don't volunteer to wear a wristband and raise awareness. Though this may be better than nothing, it doesn't address the problem she's having. Yes, your wristband may illicit a question or two from a friend…but the person who will be remembered is the person who helped in the most meaningful way. Skip the next Chipotle run and donate the ten dollars, sell something on Craigslist that's been sitting around and give the proceeds, or work some overtime and send her the money.

That may not be the easiest/most convenient approach for you, but it will have the most meaningful effect. Don't wait for the most convenient opportunity or what you think is the ideal situation. Regardless of how big/little your donation, time or introduction is that contributes to solving another's problem, if you give it your best, it will be enough and it will be appreciated.

Beyond You: A Field for the Future

Sometimes you add value to people who are a part of your day-to-day life, and sometimes your day-to-day seeds allow you the opportunity to reach people you'll never meet.

I was sitting on a plane recently next to a young researcher who'd just begun his career at UNC after grad school. I told him that my father-in-law is a biophysicist at the National Institutes of Health in Maryland, and when I mentioned his name during our conversation, my seat-neighbor knowingly smiled and said that he had read some of his research papers during grad school. It was clear to me the impact my father-in-law had created, far beyond the people in his day-to-day life.

I won't pretend to fully understand the depth of my father-in-law's body of work (in fact, the more I try to understand it the more I feel like an intellectual monkey!), but I do know that his 40+ years of research has made him a very respected man in scientific circles. And while his work has been recognized and applauded during his career, it's exciting to think that he is reaching people that he may never meet thanks to decades of diligence and effort. What will the next wave of researchers, like the young man on the plane, be able to unlock as they stand on the research of dedicated scientists, like my father-in-law?

Many times, the seeds you plant with your life produce a harvest well beyond anything you can foresee. The ripple effect of your achievements can reach people in the next generation and beyond, and the seeds you plant into the lives of others can too. Let's wrap up this chapter with a story about how the seeds you plant into relationships can produce a harvest beyond your years. Such was the case with John Quincy Adams.

John Quincy Adams, former President of the United States, was passionate in pursuing his vision of a slave-free America. He believed so deeply in the equality of men that after his term as President ended, he went *back* into the House of Represenatives to continue his fight! In the early 1840's, Adams fought vigilently for and won the freedom of 36 Africans who had killed the captain and mate of the slave ship, 'Amistad'. He proved to the Supreme Court that these men had been free men, and had been kidnapped and transported illegally across the Atlantic. In 1843, he created and proposed a three-step plan to end slavery (it was rejected). In 1844, Adams succeeded in repealing the notorious 'gag rule', which banned petition and debate over slavery in the House of Representatives. Towards the end of his life, John Quincy Adams risked his own safety to lead the anti-slavery movement in Congress.

In 1848, Adams died in the midst of his fight to abolish slavery (quite literally, as he stood up to speak as Congress was in session and suddenly fell to the ground, the victim of a stroke). He made progress in his lifetime, but sadly never lived to see his vision come to pass. However, in the last year of his life, a young congressman caught his attention. Adams saw a spark of something in him, and spent many of his final days pouring into his new friend and protégé. He mentored him and shared with him his three-part plan to end slavery and create a free America. The two became so close that this man was one of Adams' pallbearers at his funeral.

Unfortunately, the young congressman who Adams had nurtured and taught did not get re-elected to Congress the following year. In fact, he didn't win another election until 1860, when he was elected President of the United States. That young man was Abraham Lincoln.

Though Adams never lived to see his vision come true, his dream lived on through the struggle and victory of his protégé, Lincoln, who took up his dear mentor's fight for the abolition of slavery in the United States of America.

When I first heard this bit of history from David Barton and Rick Green of Wall Builders, I couldn't help but wonder—what if Adams had never planted those seeds in Lincoln? What if he had never taken the time to shape and mold this young man? How long would it have taken for The Emancipation Proclamation to come to pass? Or (and this is a sobering thought) would we still be waiting?

Relationships are powerful, both in your present life and your future career. And sometimes, the relational seeds you plant into others are so important that they will carry your purpose beyond a single lifetime.

The Field You're Standing In Today

Everything about how you interact with people is a seed. Right now, you're standing in the field that you've planted over these last years. If you don't like it, you probably can't change much this second, but you can start planting a better field for the future. If you're lonely, plant better seeds and be a friend to someone. If you're stuck, help someone else in their pursuit move on to the next level. If you want others to add to you, add value to them first.

Remember, your success in life is directly linked to those closest to you. Today, begin to add value to those people and see how much your world will change!

Embrace the fact that your seeds can create a harvest for your own life, and can produce a harvest in the lives of those around you for years to come.

Chapter Review

Create Your Life: Add Value to People

Action Items

Are there areas of want in your life? List a few.
(i.e., great friends, financial prosperity, etc.)

_____

_____

_____

How can you plant more good seeds to change your future harvest?
(i.e., be a better friend, stay connected with family consistently, start a business, invest in something, etc.)

_____

_____

_____

Who are important people in your life for whom you can do something helpful?
(i.e., parents who need help with house/tech stuff, friends you can connect to one another, new endeavors to support, etc.)

Person: _____

How you can help: _____

Person: _____

How you can help: _____

Create Your Life:
Kill What's in Front of You

Mark Nathan

I like to think I grew up in the golden age of video games. I've had a chance to play the systems that launched the era, such as Atari and Commodore 64, but the first system I ever owned was the original Nintendo. I remember opening that box on Christmas morning in 1988 and knowing my life had just changed forever. Since that defining moment, I have played every type of game on every system out there—*Super Mario Brothers/Duck Hunt* on my very first Nintendo, *Street Fighter II* on Super Nintendo, the first *Madden* football games on Sega Genesis, *Mario Kart* on N64, *Halo* on Xbox, and more.

Games like these have come a long way over the years: the graphics and realism are mind-blowing now (as are the number of buttons on the controllers)! But throughout the years, the games always follow the same general patterns, so no matter how fancy or flashy the systems get, I will rock my opponent's face and win every time!

Right now, you may be wondering why I'm pausing to take a moment of this chapter to explain to you my video-game prowess. Perhaps you're not a gamer at all, and already don't relate and/or have no idea what I'm talking about. But you've come this far—stay with me for a few more moments, because we are about to uncover one of the biggest secrets to living a successful life—one that I found hiding in one of the first games I ever played (and my very first video game love affair): *The Legend of Zelda*.

143

Leveling Out

Another equally exciting Christmas morning, years later, I sat in our family room with my brother Matthew. Outside it was snowing, but inside Matthew and I were exploring mountainous terrain as an elf-like creature named Link. Around one of the mountain bends, we found ourselves in front of a large and mysterious post that looked important and useful (though we had no idea why). But blocking our access to the post was a huge gap in the road which we were unable to get around. We were dealing with a situation we had never come across before and we were not equipped to handle it.

I was about nine years old at the time, and turned to my older brother for guidance. "How am I supposed to get over there?" We had come to what seemed to be an impossible problem, but Matthew answered in his eleven-year-old wisdom, "I guess we're not ready for this yet…"

The only reason we were exploring in the first place was that we were stuck in the Swamp Palace level and wanted to get away for a bit. We had reached the limit of what we knew how to do: we had met every person, picked up every item, and explored every area that we could access. Heading east, an entrance was blocked. Heading south, the terrain was impossible to navigate. Heading west, we saw a village that we couldn't yet enter. And now, heading north, a huge gap in the road blocked us from reaching this very important-looking post. We were stuck and had nowhere else to go.

Instinctively, my brother said, "Well, I guess we gotta beat the Swamp Palace level if we want to move on."

We didn't wonder if the game was broken or if the developers messed up. We didn't complain about how unfair the game was. It was obvious to us that there must be something to learn or an item to pick up in Level 4 that was going to give us a new level of access beyond our current limitations.

We had leveled out, so our only option was to level up.

144

When we faced the Swamp Palace problem we were trying to avoid, we received something called a hookshot, which was a weapon that would latch onto a stationary target and pull us toward it.

After we learned to use the hookshot, the gap in the mountain road wasn't a big deal anymore. The post we saw on the other side was not a mystery; it was perfectly placed to use our hookshot. Things that seemed irrelevant or confusing in previous levels now made sense and we handled future problems with ease because of our new tool, which we only got when we beat the level we were avoiding. By mastering the level we were at, we became prepared to go on to the next.

Life is pretty simple to understand when you accept that it's actually just one gigantic video game.

Life Is One Big Video Game

Not to over-simplify things, but for me, this journey through life is fundamentally a big game of *Zelda* (or *Mario*, or *Tomb Raider*, or whatever you prefer). You begin the game generally knowing what you're trying to accomplish, but you have no idea how it's all going to come together. There will be levels to get through, problems to solve, lessons to learn and villains to defeat.

You intuitively understand that the skills you start out with won't get you very far! It's paramount that you have a willingness to take some risks, give it a shot and learn along the way. Every level prepares you for the next, each lesson creates a stronger foundation and each skill you learn makes you more unstoppable. At every step, you do the best with what you've got.

Your major focus isn't what will happen four levels from now—though you know that time will come. Your focus isn't even really on the rewards at the end of the game—though you know they'll be there. Your focus is simply this: to kill what's in front of you.

Solve the problem that's in front of you. Beat the level that's in front of you. Finish the bad guy that's in front of you. Until you do that, there is no next level. You can't beat Level 11 with your Level 2 skills. You can't have Level 11 results with your Level 2 problems.

You can't have Level 11 results with your Level 2 problems.

Progressing Through Levels

In your life, if you're currently in Level 1, that's not a bad thing! You're just getting started and this is where you get to learn some of the basics. In *Mario*, the basic skills needed to beat Level 1 are running, jumping, stomping on bad guys' heads, collecting coins and avoiding things that hurt you. These are the fundamental things needed to beat the level, so these are the lessons you must learn before you can move on.

In Level 2, you build off of what you learned in Level 1. Now that you can jump, you can learn to jump off walls. Now that you know how to stomp on bad guys, you can learn to pick them up and throw them around. Now that you've collected coins, you learn what you can do with them.

The next levels introduce more helpful tools and more harmful traps. One weapon is helpful in one scenario, but another weapon is better in another. One kind of trap requires a dodging technique, while another trap requires a jumping approach. There are more skills and lessons to learn…but they all build on what you've already done.

1° Off: Levels in Life

The desire to feel like we're progressing in life is deeply wired into us. If we're going to have this innate desire to pursue progress for the rest of our life, if we're a little off in our understanding of the "Life Levels" we're progressing through, we're in for a lifetime of feeling unfulfilled.

Life Levels are not like grade-school levels. In school, at a certain age you should be at a certain grade: at eight you should be in grade school, at thirteen you should be in junior high, and at eighteen you should be graduating from high school. If you reach these check points early, it's probably because you're gifted; if you reach them late, you may feel behind. However, life levels are not necessarily tied to your age.

Life Levels don't have a set duration. In school, the year is generally nine months long with a three-month summer break. Then you're on to the next grade. Levels in life simply aren't structured like that.

Life Levels are not tied to your IQ. Someone attending an Ivy League university is not at a higher level in life because of the university name on a degree. Levels in life are not about your GPA.

Life Levels are not tied to your title. Every organization has different levels of structure and management. It's natural to think of the next promotion as the next step up the ladder, but levels in life are not about the title on your business card.

Life Levels are not tied to your income bracket. If you come out of school making $50,000/year, the next question might be: how do I get to $75,000, and then to $100,000? True, the more money you make, the better you can provide for your family, but levels in life are not about what's happening in your bank account.

There is a tendency to think of progressing through life in a very linear way, like we progressed through school. But this type of thinking is 1° off. The journey you are on is yours alone, and will require tools and skills that are unique to you. You can't compare yourself to someone else based on your GPA, income bracket, job title or how long you've been alive. Doing so makes us very focused on avoiding failure, and taking a safe, predictable route that lives inside our comfort zone.

In reality, life levels are simply about you being fully awesome. You have unique talents, gifts, dreams and desires that no one else has. You're meant to make an impact in the world that is truly special and undeniably yours. But ask yourself: are you really living in your sweet spot like you want? Are you making the difference that you want? Prospering like you want? Having the relationships that you want? Providing for your family like you want? Levels in life are about you moving closer to that version of you. Every time you reflect and take stock of your life up to a certain point, can you see huge leaps of progress, year after year? Levels in life help you develop into the best possible version of you.

Progressing through levels in life help you develop into the best possible version of you.

Life: Level 1

Most kids spend their first years in school. We know that to do well in school, you must do your homework, listen to your teachers and learn to play nice with others. But what if we looked at school differently? What if the purpose of school wasn't only to pass tests, learn various subjects and get good grades? What if we viewed school as *Life: Level 1*.

If we view school as *Life: Level 1*, then doing your homework isn't only about getting a good grade—it's about being accountable for the things you need to do. When you don't do homework, you're avoiding an important lesson about responsibility and following through on your commitments.

If we view school as *Life: Level 1*, then listening to your teacher isn't about being a teacher's pet. It's about learning to respect your elders. Maybe you don't understand why that's important now, but at a later level, that skill will become very important.

If we view school as *Life: Level 1*, then playing nice with others isn't just about sharing your toys—it's about learning to respect those around you. Working well with others is a basic principle that opens up many doors later on in life.

When you learn these lessons, it affects you more than you know. The more you do your homework, the more you prove to yourself, your parents and your teachers that you can be trusted. That's a lot bigger than the good grades you'll get.

The more you listen to your teachers, the more they can see your strengths instead of the trouble you cause. The more they see your strengths, the more they can help you capitalize on what makes you unique and special (which is a lot better than getting a detention)!

The more you respect your classmates, the more awesome every day becomes. We've spent a number of chapters talking about having awesome people in your life. Learning to have great relationships sets you up for better things in life than you'd have if you couldn't get along with anyone.

Understanding everything as a life level gives us a lens to view the lessons and rewards of our current situation.

Life: Level 2

Life: Level 2 builds on *Life: Level 1*.

In *Life: Level 1*, you proved that you're accountable to your commitments and can follow through. In *Life: Level 2*, since you've already earned your own trust, others can trust you and you can be given more responsibility. People often want to be seen by others as the go-to guy, but the reality is that *others* will never see you as responsible if you don't first prove to *yourself* that you're responsible. You can't move on to *Life: Level 2*, until you've completed *Life: Level 1*.

In *Life: Level 1*, you learned to listen to your teachers. Now in *Life: Level 2* you build on that productive teacher/student relationship and develop a mentor/protégé relationship. If you can't learn to respect the people in your life who can teach you something right now, how will you be ready when a coach appears who can take you to the championship level in your field? You must prove that you can be a good student to the teacher you have before you can be a good student to the teacher you want.

In *Life: Level 1*, you learned how to respect others. Now in *Life: Level 2*, you can learn how to effectively work with others. You can accomplish so much more with a good partnership, but it's tough to work with other people if you don't have a fundamental respect for who they are.

Life: Level 3

Life: Level 3 may require you to learn the power of positive thinking and a figure-it-out mentality because you were given more responsibility in the second level and therefore had more things to figure out. And of course you were given more responsibility in *Life: Level 2* because you learned to work hard and be accountable in *Life: Level 1*.

Life: Level 3 may require you to learn to be appreciative of other people's unique gifts, because you've seen the results of working effectively with others (Level 2) and because you learned how to respect other's differences (Level 1).

You're now creating a track record of getting stuff done. You're now viewed as someone who takes coaching well and can work effectively as a team member. This is when promotions at your job start to pop up. This is when better relationships begin to show up in your life and things begin to move forward like you always imagined!

The rewards you want in life are always unlocked by acquiring new skills. And the only way to do that is to move up from the life level you're at now.

The rewards you want in life are always unlocked by acquiring new skills.

Progressing Through Life Levels

To be very clear: none of this is meant to be a definitive or comprehensive list of the levels you'll go through. This progression can be as diverse and varied as the people that are reading it, but life levels do tend to follow a pattern regardless of industry or background. And they all require you to level up.

Level Up:
As you progress through life, you'll need to develop expertise in an industry or skill so that you can rise through the ranks and have more to offer. That often requires you to develop different levels of focus. Your pursuit of excellence will test the boundaries of your commitment. Late nights will be common and the days will blur together, but on the other side of this is promotion and accomplishment. You start to accelerate financially as a reward to unlocking a higher level of focus and commitment.

Level Up:
More advanced levels in life will require leadership and influence, which undoubtedly means that you will need to learn how to bring out the best in people and communicate effectively. To continue to grow as a leader, there are lessons of service to others, effective time management, and living in your strengths that must be learned. As your leadership qualities grow, you will begin to make an impact in your community and may secure financial rewards for your family.

Level Up:
Toward the final life levels, you will be in rarified air. You've learned how to lead leaders and produce high levels of growth/results in your field. You've made an impact in your field and have influenced productivity in your community. You've learned how to develop others who can carry on the mission and build on your foundation. You've established a family name that carries respect, and left the gift of a legacy for your children. In short, you've made a generational impact that few ever achieve.

One thing that's important to note is that it's possible to get to later levels/ rewards in life without fully learning earlier lessons. I know plenty of people who work very hard and don't think learning to work effectively with people is very important. Those people may have garnered some personal recognition and financial reward, but their results in life will level out at some point if they don't level up in the area of people skills.

Conversely, there are people who are excellent with people, but have never had a time in their life where they had to really dig deep and work out a real problem. Their results in life will level out later if they don't level up in their personal accountability and work ethic.

You must develop character, ethics and a healthy balance of humility and confidence if you are to finish strong in the levels you've reached. You can't win at the highest levels in life by avoiding things you don't like.

You can't win at the highest levels in life by avoiding things you don't like.

Challenges at Every Level

Just as there are skills to learn and small victories at every life level, there are obstacles to overcome. Some will be obvious and outwardly visible struggles, but many will be internal battles.

As you've read through these pages, Dave and I have opened up our own personal stories to share our vulnerabilities, weaknesses and character flaws that we've had to overcome. We went through mazes, acquired new tools and beat bad guys to create the life we wanted to live. We had to learn to stop avoiding pain and problems. We had to learn to take things one step at a time. We had to learn to accept the stages of boredom and drudgery. We had to learn that our life was bigger than just us.

As David moved through his life levels, he stood in front of an obstacle that blocked his path at every turn, refusing to let him move on. The obstacle? Selfishness. But when he overcame selfishness and gave up the idea that his life should revolve around him, he began to find himself. He left the gang he was involved in, devoted his life to a bigger purpose, and ended up being on national television for the service he was providing to his community.

I struggled for years trying to get past a problem that I didn't even know I had. It was so good at pointing the finger at other people that I barely realized it was there. The problem? Avoidance. Someone *else* was always to blame. But when I took personal responsibility for my character flaws and dealt with them, I was finally able to combat entitlement and disorganization in my life. Doing this allowed me to launch a film festival when I was twenty-one years old that had 300 people in attendance.

When David was hiding upstairs in his bedroom sobbing and asking God why his life was the way it was, he was actually experiencing one of the most insurmountable level-blockers of all: pain. Pain clouds your judgment and tries to convince you to focus solely on you. But David flipped pain on its head and used it as a motivator to become something more. He allowed those painful experiences to define him — but on his own terms. He became resolutely responsible and defiantly proud of who he was and from where he had come. Developing these traits ultimately put him through school and landed him a position at Goldman Sachs.

At an earlier level, I battled a vision-blocking fog that lured me in with promises of passion, pleasure, non-stop inspiration and fun. This fog was short-term thinking. Short-term thinking tried to make me focus only on things I could see clearly. Short-term thinking tried to convince me to get off paths that were difficult or challenging. In some cases, it made me decide never to start down a road at all because I didn't immediately see the end result. But when I defeated short-term thinking, I was able to fight through the fog and drudgery of doing things that I didn't like doing, and ultimately earned my financial freedom at twenty-seven years old.

And the story continues: David acquired the skill of resolve, which ultimately brought him to a job at the White House. I obtained knowledge that allowed me to develop myself in any way I desired: the knowledge

153

of how to create positive habits. Older, wiser people came into our lives and offered us valuable pieces of information to help us along our path, and partners joined us to help us fight and win our battles. And who knows what dragons and bad guys, weapons and tools, skills and abilities, and partners and mentors will join us to help defeat levels that are still to come?

To be overly transparent, I feel like I'm currently playing at Level 6 and I'm excited about one day (hopefully) getting to Level 11. Of course, global impact and generational prosperity is the end goal. But for right now, I have goals and a plan for this month and this year. In short, I need to beat the level I'm at currently.

Leveling up in life is simple: don't avoid your problems and kill what's in front of you.

How to Level Up

Leveling up in life is simple: don't avoid your problems and kill what's in front of you.

If you're struggling in school, give it everything you got. You probably won't use 85% of what you learn by the time you're five years into your career, but the real lesson you're learning is in the discipline you'll need to get it done. The same lack of discipline that keeps you awake at three in the morning cramming right before a test is the same lack of discipline that will keep you stagnant at a job down the road. Force yourself to follow your plan, and you will find that school is easier and you'll accomplish more at your job. Kill what's in front of you.

Do you find that you're habitually ten minutes late for everything? This lack of accountability will cost you opportunity (and your reputation) until you beat it. How can you do business with others or complete a project together without mutual trust? When you're late or wrong, just own it and apologize. No more excuses, justifying your actions, or placing blame on anyone other than yourself. Rebuild your confidence and reputation one opportunity at a time. Kill what's in front of you.

Do you find that you are typically pretty perfect and you have absolutely no tolerance for anyone who has ever been late in completing a task? The lesson you need to learn may involve finding grace for other people, learning to see others for their strengths and acknowledging that you have your own weaknesses. But the tricky part to all of this is that life doesn't label situations with the lessons that you're supposed to learn!

Learning how to be accountable might start with screwing up at work or breaking a promise to a friend. But instead of lying or making excuses like you may have done in the past, you own up and admit that you messed up. You apologize and work to make amends.

Learning hard work probably looks like the grunt work at your job...the calls, the research, the writing, and the nuts and bolts that no one likes to deal with. But just because you don't like it doesn't mean it's not important. Accept the fact that liking the work is not a prerequisite for doing the work. If it needs to get done, just suck it up and do it as well (and as soon) as you can.

Learning to be responsible might look like a syllabus for a difficult class that you're taking. Responsibility might look like a client at work that requires some additional hours even though you know you'll miss a few happy hours. Responsibility might also look like a $500/month gap in your family budget that requires developing an extra stream of income. You must learn to do things simply because they need to get done.

I don't know what you've been struggling with in this level of life, but I bet you do.

There is something you need to work on, something that has been an issue for you many times before, some area where you need to level up. Whatever that first thing was that popped in your head when you started reading about the levels—work ethic, discipline, financial responsibility, being accountable, disrespecting people, character, etc.—go beat it!

155

Kill what's in front you.

The great thing about life is that it doesn't give you what you hope for; it gives you what you deserve. That is the best news on the planet when you're willing to develop new skills and learn new lessons, one level at a time. You will find passion in the rewards along the way. You will find passion in everything you begin to accomplish. You will find passion as you overcome you.

Don't hope for a life of passion—create a life you're passionate about living.

Start today. Kill what's in front of you.

Chapter Review

Create Your Life: Kill What's in Front of You

Action Items

How do you need to Level Up in these different areas of your life?

Personal Life
(e.g., being lazy, being disorganized, time/financial management, etc.)

_____

_____

_____

_____

Professionally
(e.g., industry knowledge/expertise, professionalism, etc.)

_____

_____

_____

_____

In Relationships
(e.g., appreciation, communication, adding value, etc.)

_____

_____

_____

_____

Conclusion — Game On

David Anderson and Mark Nathan

We spent the first half of this book clearing up misunderstandings about what living a life of passion really looks like. Most of us have the desire to impact our families and to leave a mark on our communities. But maybe we were 1° off in our understanding of how that life was going to come together.

We had delusions about finding a life full of passion that would be without problems and pain-free, and that would fill our hearts with purpose and commitment during every moment of our lives. But now we know that we will never find a life we are passionate about; rather, we must create a life that we're passionate about.

We will never find a life we are passionate about; rather, we must create a life we're passionate about.

We spent the second half of this book talking about some of the tangible action steps you can start taking to help you create a life that builds more awesome things every day. We must be clear about what we want that life to look like (and what we don't want it to look like). We need to develop amazing relationships as well as habits, and focus on adding value everywhere we go. And we must build a life we're proud to be living, one victory at a time—which only happens when you kill what's in front of you.

Though the great authors of this world could fill encyclopedias with pearls of wisdom on what it takes to lead a successful life, the topics we've shared about in this book are, to us, some of the most important lessons that our generation can learn and embrace.

We care too much about each and every one of you reading this book to leave something out. Even as we finish writing these words, we have moved into new phases in our lives, tackled new projects, and started to experience new levels. But everything from this point forward will be built from the lessons within these pages. These chapters are some of the most fundamental truths we've learned up to this point in our lives, and we are excited to see what the next chapters hold for us all!

One Final Thought...

If you can remember this, you'll be just fine as we all move down our separate paths:

The only thing that will never change in life is that life is always changing. No matter who you are, where you are or what you've accomplished up to this point in your life, twelve months from now you will be a different person. Maybe you'll have a different job, live in a new neighborhood, or your Facebook relationship status will have changed. Even if all of the external things seem the same, you are not at that same point in life—if for no other reason than you are now one year older. There is no standing still. The truth is, you are either moving forward with time, or you are moving backward by default.

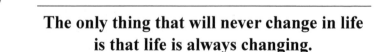

The only thing that will never change in life is that life is always changing.

One of the biggest mistakes that we can make is trying to fit the new things happening in our lives into our old ways of operating. When you learn new information, meet new people or have new opportunities show up, don't make the mistake of constantly trying to cram the new you into the old you. You need to keep up with how fast things are evolving in order to stay ahead in life. Thankfully, you probably already have experience doing this to a certain degree.

When you got to college, you had a new situation, new responsibilities, and a new lifestyle. Consciously or unconsciously, you overhauled your schedule and priorities. You didn't try and cram college into how you operated while you were in high school. Anyone who goes through college must effectively wipe the slate clean and reevaluate what the important things are in this new chapter of life.

When you graduated college and started working, you had this new thing called a job that you had to fit into your life. You didn't try and fit your work schedule into your college schedule. If you wanted to keep that new job, you had to make it a top priority and then plan around it. You readjusted your finances, habits and priorities to make that job work, and consequently to make the next chapter in your life productive.

You are either moving forward with time, or you are moving backward by default.

When people say life is hard, it often comes from the fact that they are not adapting to life as it changes. It is nearly impossible to keep fitting your new life into your old one. Life seems hard only when you haven't decided to embrace change.

When you're single, you can come and go as you please, your schedule can be whatever you'd like it to be, and an entire weekend can change at the sound of a text message. Once you get married, there is now another person with whom you are building a life. That means you coordinate schedules and communicate a lot more. Some people feel like it's a nuisance or become indignant that they have to "report in," or they feel like they are losing some of their freedom by having the "ball and chain." But being married only cramps your style if you haven't taken a second to acknowledge that you're in a new chapter of your life and communication with your spouse is how you will build an effective

161

relationship. You don't try to fit your married lifestyle into your single-guy lifestyle—because that would create a lot of problems! You wipe the slate clean and elevate this relationship in your life. You readjust your schedule, your habits and your priorities to make this next chapter of your life as successful as possible.

When you have kids, again, you wipe the slate clean, and add this new little life to the equation. You reevaluate your schedule, finances and your priorities. You don't groan and complain every time you pick them up or make them food—it's just part of life now. Whatever you need to change isn't drudgery and it's not a nuisance; it just becomes part of what you need to do to be a good parent.

If you want a concluding thought, here it is: don't fight change—embrace it.

Don't fight change—embrace it.

This book may have inspired some new thoughts. It may have challenged some of the things that you've heard and how you've started to build your life. But hopefully it has also given you some ideas for steps you can take to make this next level in your life as successful as possible.

Now that you have new information, you might be thinking about your world a bit differently. Our challenge to you is to wipe the slate clean and reevaluate what you want this next chapter of your life to look like. Where is your life going, and what do you need to do at this level of the game to make your journey everything you want it to be?

The life you're putting together will be an amazing adventure if you see it that way. There are opportunities to explore right now! There are lessons to learn from your "problems" right now! There are people who can add value to your life for a long time, and those relationships are happening right now! If you step boldly and with conviction into everything you're doing, it can and will pay off for the remainder of your life.

Living a life that you are passionate about is a reality. Don't dream it away within the delusion of passion; take the simple and practical action steps that will create a life that you are passionate about living!

We wish you constant revelation and amazing success in all of your choices. We can't wait for you to see how your grand adventure unfolds!

We'll see you at the top.